COWBOY SKILLS

COWBOY SKILLS

Roping, Riding, Hunting, and More

Edited by
STEPHEN BRENNAN

Skyhorse Publishing

Skyhorse Publishing books may be purchased in bulk at special discounts for sales promotion, corporate gifts, fund-raising, or educational purposes. Special editions can also be created to specifications. For details, contact the Special Sales Department, Skyhorse Publishing, 307 West 36th Street, 11th Floor, New York, NY 10018 or info@skyhorsepublishing.com.

Skyhorse® and Skyhorse Publishing® are registered trademarks of Skyhorse Publishing, Inc.®, a Delaware corporation.

Visit our website at www.skyhorsepublishing.com.

10 9 8 7 6 5 4 3 2 1

Library of Congress Cataloging-in-Publication Data is available on file.

Cover design by Jane Sheppard
Cover photos: Thinkstock

Print ISBN: 978-1-63450-544-4
Ebook ISBN: 978-1-63450-944-2

Printed in China

TABLE OF CONTENTS

CATTLE WAS KING BY EMERSON HOUGH

It is after the railways have come to the Plains. The Indians now are vanishing. The buffalo have not yet gone, but are soon to pass.

Until the closing days of the Civil War, the northern range was wide open domain. The grasses and the sweet waters were accessible for all men who had cows to range. The land laws still were vague, and each man could construe them much as he liked. The homestead law of 1862 worked well enough so long as there were good farming lands for homesteading—lands that would support a home and a family. This same homestead law was the only one available for use on the cattle-range. In practice it was violated thousands of times—in fact, of necessity violated by any cattle man who wished to acquire sufficient range to run a considerable herd. The great timber kings and the great cattle kings, made their fortunes out of their open contempt for the homestead law, which was designed to give all the people an even chance for a home and a farm.

Swiftly enough, here and there along all the great waterways of the northern range, ranchers, and their men filed claims on the waterfronts. For the most part the open lands were held practically under squatter's rights; the first cowman in any valley usually had his rights respected, at least for a time. These were the days of the open range. Fences had not come, nor had farms been staked out.

From the Texas there now appeared thousands of long-horned cattle.

Naturally the demand for open range steadily increased. There now began the whole complex story of leased lands and fenced lands. The frontier still offered opportunity for the bold man to reap where he had not sown. Even before the rifle-smoke had scarcely time to clear away, the methods of the East overran those of the West.

But every herd which passed north for delivery of one sort or the other advanced the education of the cowman, whether of the northern or the southern ranges. Some of the southern men began to start feeding ranges in the North, retaining their breeding ranges in the South. The demand of the great upper range for cattle seemed for the time insatiable.

To the vision of the railroad builders a tremendous potential freightage now appeared. The railroad builders began to calculate that one day they would parallel the northbound cow trail with iron trails of their own and compete with nature for the carrying of this beef. The whole swift story of all that development, while the westbound rails were crossing and crisscrossing the newly won frontier, scarce lasted twenty years. Presently we began to hear in the East of the Chisholm Trail and of the Western Trail which lay beyond it, and of many smaller and intermingling branches. We heard of Ogallalla, in Nebraska, the "Gomorrah of the Range," the first great upper market-place for distribution of cattle to the swiftly forming northern ranches. The names of new rivers came upon our maps; and beyond the first railroads we began to hear of the Yellowstone, the Powder, the Musselshell, the Tongue, the Big Horn, the Little Missouri.

The wild life, bold and carefree, coming up from the South now in a mighty surging wave, spread all over that new West which offered to the people of older lands a strange and fascinating interest. Every one on the range had money; every one was independent. Once more it seemed that man had been able to overleap the confining limitations of his life, and to attain independence, self-indulgence, ease and liberty. A chorus of Homeric, riotous mirth, as of a land in laughter, rose up all over the great range. After all, it seemed that we had a new world left, a land not yet used. We still were young! The cry arose that there was land enough for all out West. And at first the trains of white-topped wagons rivaled the crowded coaches westbound on the rails.

In consequence there came an entire readjustment of values. This country, but yesterday barren and worthless, now was covered with gold, deeper than the gold of California or any of the old placers. New securities and new values appeared. Banks did not care much for the land as security—it was practically worthless without the cattle—but they would lend money on cattle at rates which did not then seem usurious. A new system of finance came into use. Side by side with the expansion of credits went the expansion of the cattle business. Literally in hundreds of thousands the cows came north from the exhaustless ranges of the lower country.

It was a wild, strange day. But withal it was the kindliest and most generous time, alike the most contented and the boldest time, in all the history of our frontiers. There never was a better life than that of the cowman who had a good range on the Plains and cattle enough to stock his range. There never will be found a better man's country in all the world than that which ran from the Missouri up to the low foothills of the Rockies.

The lower cities took their tribute of the northbound cattle for quite a time. Wichita, Coffeyville, and other towns of lower Kansas in turn made bids for prominence as cattle marts. Agents of the Chicago stockyards would come down along the trails into the Indian Nations to meet the northbound herds and to try to divert them to this or that market as a shipping-point. The Kiowas and Comanches, not yet wholly confined to their reservations, sometimes took tribute, whether in theft or in open extortion, of the herds laboring upward through the long slow season.

Trail-cutters and herd-combers, licensed or unlicensed hangers-on to the northbound throngs of cattle, appeared along the lower trails—with some reason, occasionally; for in a great northbound herd there might be many cows included under brands other than those of the road brands registered for the drovers of that particular herd. Cattle thieving became an industry of certain value, rivaling in some localities the operations of the bandits of the placer camps. There was great wealth suddenly to be seen. The weak and the lawless, as well as the strong and the unscrupulous, set out to reap after their own fashion where they had not sown. If a grave here or there appeared along the trail or at the edge of the straggling town, it mattered little. If the gamblers and the desperadoes of the cow towns such as Newton, Ellsworth, Abilene, Dodge, furnished a man for breakfast day after day, it mattered little, for plenty of men remained, as good or better. The life was large and careless, and bloodshed was but an incident.

During the early and unregulated days of the cattle industry, the frontier insisted on its own creed, its own standards. But all the time, coming out from the East, were scores and hundreds of men of exacter notions of trade and business. The enormous waste of the cattle range could not long endure. The toll taken by the thievery of the men who came to be called range-rustlers made an element of loss which could not long be sustained by thinking men. As the Vigilantes regulated things in the mining camps, so now in slightly different fashion the new property owners on the upper range established their own ideas, their own sense of proportion as to law and order. The cattle associations, the banding together of many owners of vast herds, for mutual protection and mutual gain were a natural and logical development. Outside of these there was for a time a highly efficient corps of cattle-range Vigilantes, who shot and hanged some scores of rustlers.

It was a frenzied life while it lasted—this lurid outburst, the last flare of the frontier. Such towns as Dodge and Ogallalla offered extraordinary phenomena of unrestraint. But fortunately into the worst of these capitals of license came the best men of the new regime, and the new officers of the law, the agents of the Vigilantes, the advance-guard of civilization now crowding on the heels of the wild men of the West. In time the lights of the dance-halls and the saloons and the gambling parlors went out one by one all along the frontier. By 1885 Dodge City, a famed capital of the cow trade, which will live as long as the history of that industry is known, resigned its eminence and declared that from where the sun then stood it would be a cow camp no more! The men of Dodge knew that another day had dawned. But this was after the homesteaders had arrived and put up their wire fences, cutting off from the town the holding grounds of the northbound herds.

This innovation of barb-wire fences in the seventies had caused a tremendous alteration of conditions over all the country. It had enabled men to fence in their own water-fronts, their own homesteads. Casually, and at first without any objection filed by any one, they had included in their fences many hundreds of thousands of acres of range land to which they had no title whatever. These men—like the large-handed cow barons of the Indian Nations, who had things much as they willed in a little unnoted realm all their own—had money and political influence. And there seemed still range enough for all. If a man wished to throw a drift fence here or there, what mattered it?

Up to this time not much attention had been paid to the Little Fellow, the man of small capital who registered a brand of his own, and who with a Maverick here and there and the natural increase, and perhaps a trifle of unnatural increase here and there—had proved able to accumulate with more or less rapidity a herd of his own. Now the cattle associations passed rules that no foreman should be allowed to have or register a brand of his own. Not that any foreman could be suspected—not at all!—but the foreman who insisted on his old right to own a running iron and a registered brand was politely asked to find his employment somewhere else.

> In the early days a rancher by the name of Maverick, a Texas man, had made himself rich simply by riding out on the open range and branding loose and unmarked occupants of the free lands. Hence the term "Maverick" was applied to any unbranded animal running loose on the range. No one cared to interfere with these early activities in collecting unclaimed cattle. Many a foundation for a great fortune was laid in precisely that way. It was not until the more canny days in the North that Mavericks were regarded with jealous eyes.

The large-handed and once generous methods of the old range now began to narrow themselves. Even if the Little Fellow were able to throw a fence around his own land, very often he did not have land enough to support his herd with profit. A certain antipathy now began to arise between the great cattle owners and the small ones, especially on the upper range, where some rather bitter wars were fought—the cow kings accusing their smaller rivals of rustling cows; the small man accusing the larger operators of having for years done the same thing, and of having grown rich at it.

The cattle associations, thrifty and shifty, sending their brand inspectors as far east as the stockyards of Kansas City and Chicago, naturally had the whip hand of the smaller men. They employed detectives who regularly combed out the country in search of men who had loose ideas of mine and thine. All the time the cow game was becoming stricter and harder. Easterners brought on the East's idea of property, of low interest, sure returns, and good security. In short, there was set on once more—as there had been in every great movement across the entire West—the old contest between property rights and human independence in action. It was now once more the Frontier against the States, and the States were foredoomed to win.

The barb-wire fence, which was at first used extensively by the great operators, came at last to be the greatest friend of the Little Fellow on the range. The Little Fellow, who under the provisions of the homestead act began to push West and to depart farther and farther from the protecting lines of the railways, could locate land and water for himself and fence in both. "I've got the law back of me," was what he said; and what he said was true. Around the old cow camps of the trails, and around the young settlements which did not aspire to be called cow camps, the homesteaders fenced in land—so much land that there came to be no place near any of the shipping-points where a big herd from the South could be held. Along the southern range artificial barriers to the long drive began to be raised. It would be hard to say whether fear of Texas competition or of Texas cattle fever was the more powerful motive in the minds of ranchers in Colorado and Kansas. But the cattle quarantine laws of 1885 nearly broke up the long drive of that year. Men began to talk of fencing off the trails, and keeping the northbound herds within the fences—a thing obviously impossible.

The railroads soon rendered this discussion needless. Their agents went down to Texas and convinced the shippers that it would be cheaper and safer to put their cows on cattle trains and ship them directly to the ranges where they were to be delivered. And in time the rails running north and south across the Staked Plains into the heart of the lower range began to carry most of the cattle. So ended the old cattle trails.

What date shall we fix for the setting of the sun of that last frontier? Perhaps the year 1885 is as accurate as any—the time when the cattle trails practically ceased to bring north their vast tribute. But, in fact, there is no exact date for the passing of the frontier. Its decline set in on what day the first lank "nester" from the States outspanned his sun-burned team as he pulled up beside some sweet water on the rolling lands, somewhere in the West, and looked about him, and looked again at the land map held in his hand.

"I reckon this is our land, Mother," said he.

When he said that, he pronounced the doom of the old frontier.

THE COWBOY LIFE

RANCH WORK

On the ranch the day's business started early. At the first sign of dawn, the crusty cook gets out of his kitchen bunk, lights his fire, bawls at the horse wrangler the "roll out," and sets about preparing breakfast.

All during the night, the riding ponies had grazed in close to the house. Although the wrangler rose the moment he was called and limited his toilet to putting on his hat, the first wreath of blue smoke from the chimney already had warned the horses of impending work; and by the time the wrangler got out of doors, there was not a single pony within half a mile of the place, only the few "night horses" inside the corral.

One of them was saddled, and the scattered band of ponies was rounded up. After a quick breakfast the men carried their saddles and bridles to the corral, and in soon had the animals ready for work.

On cold days the more kindly riders held their bits before the fire a moment and shielded them by a glove or a coat flap during the transit between the inner house and the horse's mouth. They did this despite foreknowledge of their broncos' likely lack of gratitude. Each of those exasperating little brutes would stand, head hanging down, and would resignedly allow the bridle to be put atop his crown, and after a slap or two and many profane requests, the pony would lower his head and would release his viselike closed jaws, would accept the bit and busily begin champing on its roller; would take the saddle; would gaze reproachfully at his tormenter; and then apparently would doze off.

During warm weather life was comparatively easy. There were, of course, the spring and fall roundups and the resultant "drives" to the "shipping point" at the railroad.

There was the gentling of horses. If the ranch was in a region that necessitated use of a different feeding ground in winter from that of summer, the livestock would have to be shifted from one of these ranges to the other, the **winter range** being in the low country, while the **summer range** would be on the higher "benches," or on the upper levels of the hills.

There were inspection trips around the range, **outridings** to discover the location and physical state of the scattered groups of stock, to check the condition of the water and grass and to move the stock to fresh ground if it was found to be insufficient, to fend the animals away from known patches of loco-weed, to discover by **riding sign** whether any animals were straying too far afield and if so to turn them homeward, to rescue, by means of a tightly drawn lariat and straining pony some bogged, mired steer or horse, to look out for signs of thieves, settlers, and predatory animals, and if necessary, to lay traps or poisoned baits for wolves.

Diseased or injured animals were inspected, and according to the nature of the problem, were treated or destroyed.

In addition to all these incidents, there might be the work of salvage at some cloudburst's scene, a prairie fire to suppress, or an urgent call for aid against marauding Indians.

Mail had to be carried to and from the post office, perhaps a hundred miles or more away; and sometimes the wagons had to make a long trip for supplies.

These wagons, stout, springless, creaking things, traversed awful roads and country devoid of road, often taking to the boulder-strewn beds of streams, dragged on their bone-jarring, noisy way by two or more oxen. The wagons were driven by teamsters or **bull-whackers**, not by cowboys.

But the list of daily chores is not finished. Horses had to be shod, work animals on all four feet, saddle animals, if at all, on the front feet only unless they were to be used in very rocky country. In this case, they were usually shod on each of their four feet.

Repairs had to be made to saddles and to wagons. Lariats and harnesses had to be mended.

A clash with Indians was sometimes serious business. After the government had forced the Indians onto reservations and left the bulk of the plains to the ranchers, an Indian tribe occasionally "jumped" its reservation, and went on the "warpath." Cowboys were occasionally drawn into this by running afoul of the belligerent Natives, or by being taken on by the army for auxiliary service.

PRAIRIE FIRES

A prairie fire sometimes produced exciting duties. Fires were frequent; but usually of small importance—and if promptly attacked—easily exterminated. At other times, however, they were terrifying.

The two methods most often used in fighting prairie fires are **straddling** and **backfiring.** In straddling, two mounted men—one on either side—drag at lariat's end, heaps of green hides, or wet blankets along the fire line, while other men, mounted or afoot, beat at the fire's sidelines with similar tools or with bunches of brush.

The thickness of the grass or the velocity of the wind might generate heat or movement so as to make straddling impossible, and then the only remedy was to "backfire" across the burn's prospective course. Along the zone selected for the "backfire," a horsemen trailed bundles of burning sticks. The flames this started were held in check on their homeward side by straddling them.

TWISTERS

Occasionally a tornado or twister tore its way across the plains, leaving dead animals in its wake and crazed, maddened cattle tearing in wild stampede. Heavy wind, thunder, and lightning meant difficult and dangerous riding before the cowboys could get the panicked heard back into some kind of order.

The twister's prelude was awesome, and its onset was terrific. A sky of inky blackness in one quarter of the sky, suffused with tones of copper and dark green. At first whatever wind had been blowing ceased, and then fell a silence, deathlike except for the nervous lowing of the cattle. Presently came a long-drawn moaning sound, and then with a roar, a screwing, lightning-capped funnel, point down, lined with dust, bushes, and trees, rushed out of the copper and green, and tore across the flatland.

The punchers had seconds in which to act, strove to guess the funnel's prospective course and throw the cattle away from it and if possible, into protecting gullies. Despite the limited time, there was some opportunity for maneuver, because the funnel was usually of comparatively small diameter, a few hundred yards at the most. Moreover, it would occasionally hang, which is to say, would for a moment or two, slow or even halt its progress. Then, too, it might now and then skip, lift, or raise its tip from the ground and sail harmlessly until lowering itself to the earth again and resuming its murderous course.

The desperate punchers stayed with the rampaging cattle until the last possible instant, then spun their horses, facing the storm, leaning flat on their animals' necks, and charged headlong through the almost solid wall of wind that flanked the storm's funnel. Taken sideways by the wall of wind might mean a horse blown over. Taken in any position by the funnel itself almost surely meant death. Witnesses have reported cattle and horses picked up and carried more than a quarter of a mile through the air before the storm tired of her playthings and dropped them.

RANGE CATTLE

While roaming on the range, the less the cattle are interfered with, the better, particularly in winter. In this half-wild state, they can take much better care of themselves and find shelter and food; whereas, if they were herded—that is, controlled by men—they would probably starve.

The cattle split up into bunches and take possession of some small valley or slope where they can get water at no great distance. The shallowest spring bubbling up through mud will satisfy several head, if they get it all to themselves. But when you reach it, there is nothing fit for you to drink, and most likely your horse will refuse the mixture of mud in alkaline water, which pleases the cow.

If water is scarce, the cattle must make long tramps, and the country is then crossed by deeply trodden paths, which are an unerring guide to the thirsty horseman. The cattle come down these paths just before the sun gets hot, have a drink, and then lie down till the evening, when they go off again to the pasture at some distance and feed most part of the night.

WINTER WORK

In the beginning of winter, the cattle leave the high ground, and the appearance of a few hundred head in the valley which the day before was empty tells the tale of severe cold or snow storms in the mountains.

Cattle like the shelter of heavy timber, which they find along the banks of streams, and here at some rapid or at the tail of a beaver dam is their best chance for getting water. They cannot, like the horse, eat snow, nor does their instinct suggest to them to paw away that covering to reach the grass beneath. In fact, the cattle will sometimes latch on to a herd of horses, sustaining themselves by following in their footsteps.

When times are hard, the cattle will subsist on grease wood and eat almost anything, but until the young sprouts begin to shoot, there is little to find on the prairie after the snow has

covered the ground. Bare cottonwood trees line the streams. Horses will manage to keep alive on the bark of these trees, but the cattle are far less hardy than the horses. These ponies will come through the exceptional winters when 20 percent of the cattle have been lost.

Winter brings hard work upon cold ranges. Though the tasks were fewer than at other times of the year, they were strenuous. Although inspection trips and night-herding when the thermometer reads at forty degrees below zero are no fun, the stock needs to be guarded night and day no matter what.

On a large ranch, the work was performed by cowboys operating from the main buildings, and by men stationed in far-off outpost cabins—so-called line camps. These men were interchangeably called **line riders** or **outriders**, though, strictly speaking, a **line rider** had a regular beat, while an **outrider** worked anywhere.

The riders had to know where grass was plentiful and the snow above it reasonably shallow, and to constantly keep their wards shepherded within this territory, because the animals' only food was the grass, and they could only reach it by pawing through the snow. Horses could feed themselves through even

deep covering, if it was powdery; but let an ice crust form, and the story would be very different. A thaw, immediately followed by a freeze, spelled disaster on the Range.

Even in snowless stretches, danger lurked, for rain, promptly followed by a drop in temperature, turned each grass blade into an icicle so armored that the livestock would not eat it.

The winds, however cold, were friendly to the stock in that they swept away the snow from wide stretches of grazing-ground.

Although during the winter the horse herd could take charge of itself and needed little guidance, the cattle throughout that period needed constant care.

At the sign of an impending storm—day or night—off went the riders to hustle their charges behind the protection of trees or projecting rocks, or else into valleys or swales, which were less likely to be buried deep in snow.

MEALS

At the most ranches, owners and employees ate at the same table, and in seating themselves made no distinction between wage-earner and wage-payer beyond that the seat at the table's head commonly was ceded to whichever of the owners was regarded as the leader among themselves. A few establishments set a separate table for employees, and so created some little resentment in a region where democracy was very potent.

Meals usually were of short duration, for the westerner was not formal about his eating, and did not interrupt it with conversation. In addition, the cook was impatient to do the dish-washing—and privileged by his position to speak his mind—he usually exhorted dawdlers to "swallow and git out." Meals ordinarily were promptly attended, as tardy eaters of most of the ranches received from the cook only a grin, an airy pointing at the bean-pot, and the words: "Beans, help yourselves."

The meal over, everybody returned to work—if it was midday—or if it was evening, more conversation or singing.

COW PONIES

Cow ponies are rather small animals, and half disappear under the big saddles of the cowboys, which often weigh forty pounds.

The progenitor of the cow pony was the bronco, which came into the Great Plains with the cattle driven up from Texas. They were, however, much improved in latter years. The biggest are by no means the best. A short and compact pony of about fourteen hands works more quickly than a larger animal.

Some of them, with their small and well-shaped heads and bright eyes, are really comely animals. Their manes and coats are shaggy, showing coarse breeding, and their tempers are not always to be trusted. Each hand, when out cow-punching, rides from six to ten horses, using each in turn, and without a second thought, riding one horse fifty or sixty miles.

After the day's work he takes off the saddle and the bridle, and without further ado lets the horse loose. The pony, after a good roll in the dust, takes up the scent and rejoins the herd of horses. His turn for work will not come around again for a few days.

Of course, they get nothing to eat but the grass they pick up, and they are seldom shod. Their half-wild origin is attested by the majority of duns and sorrels. The heavy saddles were believed to be a benefit to the horse, as on account of their size and solidity, they distribute the weight of the rider and his kit over a larger portion of the animal's back. There is truth in this, and on long journeys the ease of the big saddle more than compensates for the extra weight.

In roping cattle the heavy saddle is an absolute necessity. There are often two girths. These must be well tightened, and even then the jerks try the horses severely.

The end of the rope is held fast by a turn around the horn, which stands six inches above the pommel. Often the rider has to hang heavily over the farther side to prevent the whole saddle being turned round. The big spurs do not seem to hurt the horses, and to make them effective at all, the cowboy reaches his heels forward and spurs his horse in the shoulder.

CAMPING OUT

If a cowboy were starting out alone on a trip that required him to camp overnight, he'd wrap most of what he needed into the folds of his slicker and tie it behind his saddle. These necessities would be some flour, bacon, coffee, salt, a little baking powder, a can of tomatoes, and a frying pan.

When it was time to stop for the night, camp was made where forage and drinkable water were present. But the water, though drinkable, was not always pleasant. It might taste a little of sheep, contain the carcass of a steer, or be girt by banks marked with the telltale white of alkali. It might be warm and stale, or so full of sand as to demand an admixture of juice from a cactus leaf before showing clearness. But willpower, hard-boiling, and a cactus leaf were used to do away with the worst of the dangers, and water full of floating sand might easily be strained through a bandana. Thus the old cowboy saying that he "drank his cold water hot."

Occasionally, in the desert, water was nonexistent, or else so full of alkaline as hopelessly to "rust the boilers" of whoever drank it. In that case—although the horse was left to slurp the biting fluid and run the risk of being "alkalied,"—the

man might think on his canned tomatoes. The liquid portion of the can's contents assuaged thirst and counteracted the effect of the already swallowed alkali dust, while the solid vegetable wiped across his face would heal the bleeding cuts that the cannibalistic dust had made. A tomato might even occasionally be pressed against his pony's lips for their comforting.

Pitching camp was a simple process. It consisted of stripping the saddle and bridle from the horse, of turning him to graze either at the end of a picket rope or within the grip of hobbles, and finally of building a fire. Lighting the fire was not always an easy matter, for matches might be wet or lost. Then it would call for powder from a dissected cartridge, and the igniting of it by a pistol-shot.

If, as was usually the case, the coffee was unground, its beans were mashed on a rock with the butt of a pistol. The resultant mixture of vegetable and mineral substance was set aside until the frying pan should have cooked first bread and next, the bacon.

The bread would be quite eatable. A thick batter, spread thinly over the bottom of the pan, was laid upon hot coals for a moment and until a lower crust began to form. Then, tipped on edge, it was held far enough from the fire for a little heat to reach it and to raise the loaf. This achieved, the pan, still on edge, was settled for baking in the coals, and was left there until done.

This baked bread, the historic "frying pan bread" of the old west was dumped from the pan, and in went the chunks of bacon. When these had been fried, the pan was rapped against a rock or tree, to expel whatever grease as readily would come off, and then received a little water and the coffee-gravel mixture. When the boiling fluid was fairly well covered with fat melted from the utensil's insides, the beverage was ready for consumption.

The menu of the puncher on his travels was rarely more extensive than the one described above. A packhorse, when there was one, indicated quantity rather than variety of food. But it did at least insure the presence of a coffeepot.

For sleeping, the lee side of a rock or bush, the saddle for a pillow, the slicker and horse blanket for a covering, a pile of wood for replenishing the fire, collectively made the bedroom and its furnishings.

Tents and extra bedding were almost unknown even in winter. In cold weather the puncher, when afield, customarily took his horse's bridle to bed with him, so that the bit might be kept warm and the horse be spared the pain which mouthing frigid metal would have caused.

Camping in colder climates was often a trying process marked by a nocturnal contest between the desire to sleep and rheumatic pains, a contest won or lost according to how good the sleepy cowboy was at keeping his fire fueled.

A THEODORE ROOSEVELT ROUNDUP

During the wintertime there is ordinarily but little work done among the cattle. There is some line riding, and a continual lookout is kept for the very weak animals—

usually cows and calves, who have to be driven in, fed, and housed; but most of the stock are left to shift for themselves, undisturbed.

The bulk of the work is done during the summer, including the late spring and early fall, and consists mainly in a succession of roundups, beginning, with us, in May and ending toward the last of October.

Still more important is the "trail" work; cattle, while driven from one range to another, or to a shipping point for beef, are said to be "on the trail." For years, the oversupply from the vast breeding ranches to the south, especially in Texas, has been driven northward in large herds, either to the shipping towns along the great railroads, or else to the fattening ranges of the Northwest; it having been found, so far, that while the calf crop is larger in the South, beeves become much heavier in the North. Such cattle, for the most part, went along tolerably well-marked routes or trails, which became, for the time being, of great importance, flourishing—and extremely lawless—towns growing up along them; but with the growth of the railroad system, and above all with the filling-up of the northern ranges, these trails have steadily become of less and less consequence, though many herds still travel them on their way to the already crowded ranges of western Dakota and Montana, or to the Canadian regions beyond. The trail work is something by itself. The herds may be on the trail several months, averaging fifteen miles or less a day. The cowboys accompanying each have to undergo much hard toil, of a peculiarly same and wearisome kind, on account of the extreme slowness with which everything must be done, as trail cattle should never be hurried. The foreman of a trail outfit must be not only a veteran cowhand, but also a miracle of patience and resolution.

Roundup work is far less irksome, there being an immense amount of dash and excitement connected with it; and once the cattle are on the range, the important work is done during the roundup. On cow ranches, or wherever there is breeding stock, the spring roundup is the great event of the season, as it is then that the bulk of the calves are branded. It usually lasts six weeks, or thereabouts; but its end by no means implies rest for the stockman. On the contrary, as soon as it is over, wagons are sent to work out-of-the-way parts of the country that have been passed over, but where cattle are supposed to have drifted; and by the time these have come back, the first beef roundup has begun, and thereafter beeves are steadily gathered and shipped, at least from among the larger herds, until cold weather sets in; and in the fall there is another roundup, to brand the late calves and see that the stock is got back on the range. As all of these roundups are of one character, a description of the most important, taking place in the spring, will be enough.

In April we begin to get up the horses. Throughout the winter very few have been kept for use, as they are then poor and weak, and must be given grain and hay if they are to be worked. The men in the line camps need two or three apiece, and each man at the home ranch has a couple more; but the rest are left out to shift for themselves, which the tough, hardy little fellows are well able to do. Ponies can pick up a living where cattle die; though the scanty feed, which they may have to uncover by pawing off the snow, and the bitter weather often make them look very gaunt by springtime. But the first warm rains bring up the green grass, and then all the livestock gain flesh with wonderful rapidity. When the spring roundup begins, the horses should be as fat and sleek as possible.

After running free all winter, even the most sober pony is apt to betray an inclination to buck; and, if possible, we like to ride every animal once or twice before we begin to do real work with him. Animals that have escaped for any length of time are almost as bad to handle as if they had never been broken.

The stock-growers of Montana, of the western part of Dakota, and even of portions of extreme northern Wyoming—that is of all the grazing lands lying in the basin of the Upper Missouri, have united, and formed themselves into the great Montana Stock-growers' Association. Among the countless benefits they have derived from this course, not the least has been the way in which the various roundups work in with and supplement one another. At the spring meeting of the

association, the entire territory, including perhaps a hundred thousand square miles, is mapped out into roundup districts, which generally are changed only slightly from year to year.

Thus the stockmen along the Yellowstone have one roundup; we along the Little Missouri have another; and the country lying between, through which the Big Beaver flows, is almost equally important to both. Accordingly, one spring, the Little Missouri roundup, beginning May 25, and working downstream, was timed so as to reach the mouth of the Big Beaver about June 1, the Yellowstone roundup beginning at that date and place. Both then worked up the Beaver together to its head, when the Yellowstone men turned to the west and we bent back to our own river; thus the bulk of the strayed cattle of each were brought back to their respective ranges. Our own roundup district covers the Big and Little Beaver creeks, which rise near each other, but empty into the Little

Missouri nearly 150 miles apart, and so much of the latter river as lies between their mouths.

The captain or foreman of the roundup, upon whom very much of its efficiency and success depends, is chosen beforehand. He is, of course, an expert cowman, thoroughly acquainted with the country; and he must also be able to command and to keep control of the wild rough-riders he has under him—a feat needing both tact and firmness.

At the appointed day, all meet at the place from which the roundup is to start. Each ranch has most work to be done in its own roundup district, but it is also necessary to have representatives in all those surrounding it. A large outfit may employ a dozen cowboys, or over, in the home district, and yet have nearly as many more representing its interest in the various ones adjoining. Smaller outfits generally club together to run a wagon and send outside representatives, or else go along with their stronger neighbors, they paying part of the expenses.

A large outfit, with a herd of twenty thousand cattle or more can, run a roundup entirely by itself, and is able to act independently of outside help; it is therefore at a great advantage compared with those that can take no step effectively without their neighbors' consent and assistance.

If the starting-point is some distance off, it may be necessary to leave home three or four days in advance. Before this we have gotten everything ready; have overhauled the wagons, shod any horse whose forefeet are tender—as a rule, all our ponies go barefooted—and left things in order at the ranch. Our outfit may be taken as a sample of every one else's. We have a stout four-horse wagon to carry the bedding and the food; in its rear a mess-chest is rigged to hold the knives, forks, cans, etc. All our four team-horses are strong, willing animals, though of no great size, being originally just "broncos," or unbroken native horses, like the others. The teamster is also cook: a man who is a first-rate hand at both driving and cooking—and our present teamster is both—can always command his price. Besides our own men, some cowboys from neighboring ranches and two or three representatives from other roundup districts are always along, and we generally have at least a dozen "riders" as they are termed—that is, cowboys, or "cow-punchers," who do the actual cattle-work—with the wagon. Each of these has a string of eight or ten ponies. There are two herders, known as "horse-wranglers"—one for the day and one for the night. Occasionally there will be two wagons, one to carry the bedding and one the food, known, respectively, as the bed and the mess wagon; but this is not usual.

While traveling to the meeting-point, the pace is always slow, as it is important to bring the horses on the ground as fresh as possible. Accordingly we keep at a walk almost all day, and the riders assist the wranglers in driving the saddle-band, three or four going in front, and others on the side, so that the horses walk. There is always some trouble with the animals at the starting out, and they are very fresh and are restive under the saddle. The herd is likely to stampede, and any beast that is frisky or vicious is sure to show its worst side. To do really effective cow-work a pony should be well broken; but many, even of the old ones, have vicious traits, and almost every man will have in his string one or two young horses, hardly broken at all. Thanks to the rough methods of breaking on the plains, many of the so-called broken animals retain bad habits, the most common being that of bucking. Of the sixty odd horses on my ranch, all but half a dozen were broken by ourselves; and though my men are all good riders, a good rider is not necessarily a good horse-breaker.

In riding these wild, vicious horses, and in careering over such very bad ground, especially at night, accidents are always occurring. A man who is merely an ordinary rider is certain to have a pretty hard time. However, everyone falls from or with his horse now and then in the cow country; and even my men, good riders though they are, are sometimes injured. One of them once broke his ankle; another a rib; another was on one occasion stunned, remaining unconscious for some hours; and yet another had certain of his horses buck under him so hard and long as finally to hurt his lungs and make him cough blood. Fatal accidents occur annually in almost every district, especially if there is much work to be done among stampeded cattle at night.

For bedding, each man has two or three pairs of blankets, and a tarpaulin or small wagon-sheet. Usually, two or three sleep together. Even in June the nights are generally cool and pleasant, and it is chilly in the early morning; although this is not always so, and when the weather stays hot and mosquitoes are plenty, the hours of darkness, even in midsummer, seem painfully long. In the Bad Lands proper, we are not often bothered very seriously by these winged pests; but in the low bottoms of the Big Missouri, and beside many of the reedy ponds and great sloughs out on the prairie, they are a perfect scourge. During the very hot nights, when they are especially active, the bedclothes make a man feel absolutely smothered, and yet his only chance for sleep is to wrap himself tightly up, head and all; and even then some of the pests will usually force their way in. At sunset I have seen the mosquitoes rise up from the land like a dense cloud, to make the hot, stifling night one long torture; the horses would neither lie down nor graze, traveling restlessly to and fro till daybreak, their bodies streaked and bloody, and the insects settling on them so as to make them all one color, a uniform gray; while the men, after a few hours' tossing about in the vain attempt to sleep, rose, built a little fire of damp sage brush, and thus endured the misery as best they could until it was light enough to work.

But if the weather is fine, a man will never sleep better nor more pleasantly than in the open air after a hard day's work on the roundup; nor will an ordinary shower or gust of wind disturb him in the least, for he simply draws the tarpaulin over his head and goes on sleeping. But now and then we have a windstorm that might better be called a whirlwind and has to be met very differently; and two or three days or nights of rain insure the wetting of the blankets, and therefore shivering discomfort.

At the meeting-place there is usually a delay of a day or two to let everyone come in; and the plain on which the encampment is made becomes a scene of great bustle and turmoil. The heavy four-horse wagons jolt in from different quarters, the horse-wranglers rushing madly to and fro in the endeavor to keep the different saddle-bands from mingling, while the cowboys with each wagon jog along in a body. The representatives from outside districts ride in singly or by twos and threes, every man driving before him his own horses, one of them loaded with his bedding. Each wagon wheels out of the way into some camping-place not too near the others, the bedding is tossed out on the ground, and then every one is left to do what he wishes, while the different wagon bosses, or foremen, seek out the captain of the roundup to learn what his plans are.

On such a day, when there is no regular work, there will often also be horse races, as each outfit is pretty sure to have

some running pony which it believes can outpace any other. These contests are always short-distance dashes, for but a few hundred yards. Horse racing is a mania with most plainsmen.

Besides the horse races, which are, of course, the main attraction, the men at a roundup will often get up wrestling matches or footraces. After the monotony of a long winter, the cowboys look forward to the roundup, where the work is hard, but exciting and varied. There is no eight-hour law in cowboy land: during roundup time we count ourselves lucky if we get off with much less than sixteen hours; but the work is done in the saddle, and the men are spurred on all the time by the desire to outdo one another in feats of daring and skillful horsemanship. There is very little quarreling or fighting; and though the fun often takes the form of rather rough horseplay, the practice of carrying dangerous weapons makes cowboys show far more rough courtesy to one another, and far less rudeness to strangers than is the case among, for instance, miners, or even lumbermen. When a quarrel may very probably result fatally, a man thinks twice before going into it, and will treat one another with a certain amount of consideration and politeness. The moral tone of a cow-camp, indeed, is rather high than otherwise. Meanness, cowardice, and dishonesty are not tolerated. There is a high regard for truthfulness and keeping one's word, intense contempt for any kind of hypocrisy, and a hearty dislike for a man who shirks his work.

The method of work is simple. The mess-wagons and loose horses, after breaking camp in the morning, move on in a straight line for some few miles, going into camp again before midday; and the day herd—consisting of all the cattle that have been found far off their range, and which are to be brought back there, and of any others that it is necessary to gather— follows on afterward. Meanwhile the cowboys scatter out and drive in all the cattle from the country round about, going perhaps ten or fifteen miles back from the line of march, and meeting at the place where camp has already been pitched. The wagons always keep some little distance from one another, and the saddle-bands do the same, so that the horses may not get mixed.

In the morning the cook is preparing breakfast long before the first glimmer of dawn. As soon as it is ready, probably about three o'clock, he utters a long-drawn shout, and all the sleepers bundle out, rubbing their eyes and yawning, draw on their boots and trousers—if they have taken the latter off—roll up and cord their bedding, and usually without any attempt at washing, crowd over to the little smoldering fire. The men are rarely very hungry at breakfast, and it has to be eaten in shortest order. Each man, as he comes up, grasps a tin cup and plate from the mess-box, pours out his tea or coffee, with sugar, helps himself to one or two of the biscuits that have been baked in a Dutch oven, and perhaps also to a slice of the fat pork swimming in the grease of the frying pan, ladles himself out some beans, if there are any, and squats down on the ground to eat his breakfast. The meal is not an elaborate one; nevertheless a man will have to hurry if he wishes to eat it before hearing the foreman sing out, "Come, boys, catch your horses." The night wrangler is now bringing in the saddle-band, which he has been up all night guarding. A rope corral is rigged up by stretching a rope from each wheel of one side of the wagon, making a V-shaped space, into which the saddle-horses are driven. Certain men stand around to keep them inside, while the others catch the horses: many outfits have one man to do all the roping. As soon as each has caught his horse—usually a strong, tough animal, the small, quick ponies being reserved for the work round the herd in the afternoon—the band, now in the charge of the day wrangler, is turned loose, and everyone saddles up as fast as possible. It still lacks some time of being sunrise, and the air has in it the chill of the early morning. When all are saddled, many of the horses bucking and dancing about, the riders from the different wagons all assemble where the captain is sitting, already mounted. He waits a very short time before announcing the proposed camping-place and parceling out the work among those present. If, as is often the case, the line of march is along a river or creek, he appoints some man to take a dozen others and drive down (or up) it ahead of the day herd; the day herd itself is driven and guarded by a dozen men detached for that purpose. The rest of the riders are divided into two bands, placed under men who know the country, and start out, one on each side, to bring in every head for fifteen miles back.

The two bands, a score of riders in each, separate and make their way in opposite directions. The leader of each tries to get such a "scatter" on his men that they will cover completely all the land gone over. This morning work is called circle riding, and is peculiarly hard in the Bad Lands on account of the remarkably broken nature of the country. The men come in on lines that tend to a common center—as if the sticks of a fan were curved. As the band goes out, the leader from time to time detaches one or two men to ride down through certain sections of the country, making the shorter, or what are called inside, circles, while he keeps on; and finally, retaining as companions the two or three whose horses are toughest, makes the longest or outside circle himself, going clear back to the divide, or whatever the point may be that marks the limit of the roundup work, and then turning and working straight to the meeting-place. Each man, brings in every head of cattle he can find.

Sometimes we trot or pace, and again we lope or gallop; the few who are to take the outside circle must ride both hard and fast. Although only grass-fed, the horses are tough and wiry; but are each used only once in four days, or thereabouts,

so they stand the work well. The course out lies across great
grassy plateaus, along knifelike ridge crests, among winding
valleys and ravines, and over acres of barren, sun-scorched
buttes, that look grimly grotesque and forbidding, while in
the Bad Lands, the riders unhesitatingly go down and over
places where it seems impossible that a horse should even
stand. The line of horsemen will quarter down the side of a
butte, where every pony has to drop from ledge to ledge like a
goat, and will go over the shoulder of a soapstone cliff, when
wet and slippery, with a series of plunges and scrambles that,
if unsuccessful, would land horses and riders in the bottom
of the washout below. In descending a clay butte after a rain,
the pony will put all four feet together and slide down to the
bottom almost on his haunches.

When the men on the outside circle have reached the bound
set to them—whether it is a low divide, a group of jagged
hills, the edge of the rolling, limitless prairie, or the long,
waste reaches of alkali and sage brush—they turn their horses'
heads and begin to work down the branches of the creeks,
one or two riding down the bottom, while the others keep
off to the right and left, a little ahead and fairly high up on the
side hills, so as to command as much of a view as possible.

On the level or rolling prairies the cattle can be seen a long way off, and it is an easy matter to gather and to drive them; but in the Bad Lands, every little pocket, basin, and coulee has to be searched, every gorge or ravine entered, and in the dense patches of brushwood and spindling, wind-beaten trees closely examined. All the cattle are carried on ahead down the creek; and it is curious to watch the different behavior of the different breeds. A cowboy riding off to one side of the creek, and seeing a number of long-horned Texans grazing in the branches of a set of coulees, has merely to ride across the upper ends of these, uttering the drawn-out "ei-koh-h-h" so familiar to the cattle-men, and the long-horns will stop grazing, stare fixedly at him, and then, wheeling, strike off down the coulees at a trot, tails in air, to be carried along by the center riders. Our own range cattle are not so wild, but nevertheless are easy to drive, while Eastern-raised beasts have little fear of a horseman, and merely stare stupidly at him until he rides directly at them. Every little bunch of stock is thus collected, and all are driven along together. At the place where some large fork joins the main creek, another band may be met, driven by some of the men who have left earlier in the day to take one of the shorter circles; and thus, before coming down to the bottom where the wagons are camped and where the actual "roundup" itself is to take place, this one herd may include a couple of thousand head; or, on the other hand, the longest ride may result in finding only a dozen animals. As soon as the riders are in, they disperse to their respective wagons to get dinner and change horses, leaving the cattle to be held by one or two of their number. If only a small number of cattle have been gathered, they will all be run into one herd; if there are many of them, the different herds will be held separate.

The plain where a roundup is to take place offers a picturesque sight. I well remember one such. It was on a level bottom in a bend of the river, which here made an almost semicircular sweep. The bottom was in the shape of a long oval, hemmed in by an unbroken line of steep bluffs so that it looked like an amphitheater. The wagons were camped among the cotton wood trees fringing the river, a thin column of smoke rising up from beside each. In the great round corral,

toward one end, the men were already branding calves, while the whole middle of the bottom was covered with lowing herds of cattle and shouting, galloping cowboys.

As soon as, or even before, the last circle riders have come in and have snatched a few hasty mouthfuls to serve as their midday meal, they begin to work the herd, or herds. The animals are held in a compact bunch, most of the riders forming a ring outside, while a couple from each ranch successively look the herds through and cut out those marked with their own brand. It is difficult in such a moving mass but to find all of one's own animals; a man must have natural gifts, as well as considerable experience, before he becomes a good brand-reader and is able really to "clean up a herd"— that is, be sure he has left nothing of his own in it.

To do good work in cutting out from a herd, not only should the rider be a good horseman, but he should also have a skillful, thoroughly trained horse. A good cutting pony is not common, and is generally too valuable to be used anywhere but in the herd.

When looking through the herd, it is necessary to move slowly; and when any animal is found, it is taken to the outskirts at a walk. Once at the outside, however, the cowboy has to ride like lightning; for as soon as the beast he is after finds itself separated from its companions, it endeavors to break back among them, and a young, range-raised steer or heifer runs like a deer. In cutting out a cow and a calf, two men work together. As the animals of a brand are cut out, they are held apart by some rider detailed for the purpose, who is said to be "holding the cut."

All this time the men holding the herd have their hands full, for some animal is always trying to break out, when the nearest man flies at it at once, and after a smart chase, brings it back to its fellows. As soon as all the gathered cows and calves have been cut out, the rest are driven clear of the ground and turned loose because they are headed in a direction contrary to that to be traveled the following day. Then the riders surround the next herd, the men holding cuts move them up near it, and the work is begun anew.

If it is necessary to throw an animal, either to examine a brand or for any other reason, half a dozen men will have their ropes out at once; and then it is spur and quirt in a rivalry to see who can outdo the other until the beast is roped and thrown. A first-class hand will, unaided, rope, throw, and tie down a cow or steer in a short time.

Usually however, one man ropes the animal by the head and another gets the loop of his lariat around one or both its hind legs, and then it is twisted over and stretched out. In following an animal on horseback, the man keeps steadily swinging the rope round his head, by a dexterous motion of the wrist only, until it is time to throw it. When on foot, especially if catching horses in a corral, the loop is dragged loosely on the ground. A good roper will hurl out the coil with accuracy and force; it whistles through the air, and settles round the object with a nearly infallible certainty. Mexicans make the best ropers; but some Texans are very little behind them. A good horse takes as much interest in the work as does his rider, and the instant the noose settles over the cow, wheels and braces himself to meet the shock, planting his legs firmly, and the steer or cow is thrown with a jerk. An unskillful rider and untrained horse will often themselves be thrown when the strain comes.

Sometimes an animal—usually a cow or steer, but strangely enough, very rarely a bull—will get fighting mad, and turn on the men. If on the drive, such a beast usually is simply dropped out; but if there is time, nothing delights the cowboys more than an encounter of this sort. Often such an animal will make a very vicious fight, and is most dangerous.

As soon as all the brands of cattle are worked, and the animals that are to be driven along have been put in the day herd, attention is turned to the cows and calves, which are already gathered in different bands, consisting each of all the cows of a certain brand and all the calves that are following them. The irons are heated, and a dozen men dismount to "wrestle" the calves. The best two ropers go in on their horses to catch them, one man keeps tally, a couple put on the brands, and the others seize, throw, and hold the little unfortunates. A first-class roper invariably catches the calf by both hind feet, and then, having taken a twist with his lariat round the horn of the saddle, drags the bawling creature, extended at full-length, up to the fire, where it is held. A less skillful roper catches round the neck, and then, if the calf is a large one, the man who seizes it has his hands full, as the bleating, bucking animal develops astonishing strength, and resists with all its power. If there are seventy or eighty calves in a corral, the scene is one of the greatest confusion. The ropers, spurring and checking

the fierce little horses, drag the calves up so quickly that a dozen men can hardly hold them; the men with the irons, blackened with soot, run to and fro; the calf-wrestlers, grimy with blood, dust, and sweat, work like beavers, while the voice of the tally-man shouts out the number and sex of each calf.

Now and then an old cow turns vicious and puts every one out of the corral. Or a maverick bull—that is, an unbranded bull—a yearling or a two-year-old, is caught, thrown, and branded. When he is let up, there is sure to be a fine scatter. Down goes his head, and he bolts at the nearest man, who gets out of the way at top speed, amid roars of laughter from all of his companions; while the men holding down calves swear savagely as they dodge charging mavericks, trampling horses, and taut ropes with frantic, plunging little beasts at the farther ends.

Every morning certain riders are detached to drive and to guard the day herd, which is most monotonous work, the men being on from four in the morning till eight in the evening. Their only rest coming at dinnertime, when they change horses. When the herd has reached the campground, there is nothing to do but to loll listlessly over the saddle in the blazing sun and watch the cattle feed and sleep, seeing that they do not spread out too much. Plodding slowly along on the trail through the columns of dust stirred up by the hoofs is not much better. Cattle travel best and fastest strung out in long lines; the swiftest taking the lead in single file, while the weak and the lazy, the young calves and the poor cows, crowd together in the rear. Two men travel along with the leaders, one on each side, to point them in the right direction; one or two others keep the flanks, and the rest are in the rear to act as "drag-drivers" to hurry up the phalanx of reluctant weaklings. If the foremost of the string travels too fast, one rider will go along on the trail a little ahead, to slow them a bit, so that those in the rear will not be left behind.

Generally all this is very tame and irksome, but by fits and starts there will be little flurries of excitement. Two or three of the circle riders may unexpectedly come over a butte nearby with a bunch of cattle, which at once start for the day herd, and then there will be a few minutes furious riding to keep them out. Or the cattle may begin to run, and then begin "milling"—that is, all crowd together into a mass wherein they move round and round, and refuse to leave it. The only way to start them is to force one's horse in among them and cut out some of their number, which then begin to travel off by themselves, when the others will probably follow. But in spite of occasional incidents of this kind, day herding has a dreary sameness about it that makes the men dislike and seek to avoid it.

From eight in the evening till four in the morning, the day herd becomes a night herd. Each wagon in succession undertakes to guard it for a night, dividing the time into watches of two hours apiece, a couple of riders taking each watch. This is generally chilly and tedious; but at times it is accompanied by intense excitement and danger, when the cattle become stampeded, whether by storm or otherwise. The first and the last watches are those chosen by preference; the others are disagreeable, the men having to turn out cold and sleepy, in the darkness—the two hours of chilly wakefulness completely breaking the night's rest. The first guards have to bed the cattle down, though the day-herders often do this themselves. This consists in hemming all their charges into as small a space as possible, and then riding round them until they lie down and fall asleep. Often this takes some time— the cattle will keep rising and lying down again. When at last most of them have become quiet, some perverse brute of a steer will deliberately hook them all up, and long strings of animals will suddenly start out from the herd at a walk. These are turned back by the nearest cowboy, only to break out at a new spot. When finally they have lain down and are chewing their cud or slumbering, the two night guards ride around them, often on very dark nights, calling or singing to them, as the sound of the human voice on such occasions seems to quiet them. In inky-black weather, especially when rainy, it is difficult and unpleasant work. Usually the watch passes off without incident, but on rare occasions the cattle become restless and prone to stampede. Anything may then start them—the plunge of a horse, the sudden approach of a coyote, or the arrival of some outside steers or cows that have smelled them and come up. Every animal in the herd will be on its feet in an instant, as if by an electric shock, and off with a rush, horns and tail up. Then, no matter how rough the ground nor how pitchy black the night, the cowboys must ride for all there is in them and spare neither their own nor their horses' necks.

Perhaps their charges break away and are lost altogether; perhaps, by desperate galloping, they may head them off, get them running in a circle, and finally stop them. Once stopped, they may break again, and possibly divide up, one cowboy, perhaps, following each band. I have known six such stops and renewed stampedes to take place in one night, the cowboy staying with his ever-diminishing herd of steers until daybreak, when he managed to get them under control again, and by careful humoring of his jaded, staggering horse, finally brought those that were left back to the camp, several miles distant. The riding in these night stampedes is wild and dangerous, especially if the man gets caught in the rush of the beasts. It also usually necessitates an immense amount of work in collecting the scattered animals.

On one such occasion, a small party of us were thirty-six hours in the saddle, dismounting only to change horses or to eat. We were almost worn out at the end of the time; but it must be kept in mind that for a long spell of such work, a stock saddle is far less tiring than the ordinary Eastern or English one, and in every way superior to it.

By very hard riding, such a stampede may sometimes be prevented. Once we were bringing a thousand head of young cattle down to my lower ranch, and as the river was high, were obliged to take the inland trail. The third night we were forced to make a dry camp, the cattle having had no water since the morning. Nevertheless, we got them bedded down without difficulty, and one of the cowboys and myself stood first guard. But very soon after nightfall, when the darkness had become complete, the thirsty brutes of one accord got on their feet and tried to break out. The only salvation was to keep them close together, as, if they once got scattered, we knew they could never be gathered; so I kept on one side, and the cowboy on the other, and never in my life did I ride so hard.

In the darkness I could but dimly see the shadowy outlines of the herd, as with whip and spurs I ran the pony along its edge, turning back the beasts at one point barely in time to wheel and keep them in at another. The ground was cut up by numerous little gullies, and each of us got several falls, horses and riders turning complete somersaults. We were dripping with sweat, and our ponies quivering and trembling like quaking aspens, when, after more than an hour of the most violent exertion, we finally got the herd quieted again.

On another occasion while with the roundup, we were spared an excessively unpleasant night only because there happened to be two or three great corrals not more than a mile or so away. All day long it had been raining heavily, and we were well drenched; but toward evening it lulled a little, and the day herd, a very large one, of some two thousand head, was gathered on an open bottom. We had turned the horses loose, and in our oilskin slickers cowered, soaked and comfortless, under the lee of the wagon, to take a meal of damp bread and lukewarm tea, the sizzling embers of the fire having about given up the ghost after a fruitless struggle with the steady downpour. Suddenly the wind began to come in quick, sharp gusts, and soon a regular blizzard was blowing, driving the rain in stinging level sheets before it. Just as we were preparing to turn into bed, with the certainty of a night of more or less chilly misery ahead of us, one of my men, an iron-faced personage, whom no one would ever have dreamed had a weakness for poetry, looked toward the plain where the cattle were, and remarked, "I guess there's 'racing and chasing on Cannobie Lea' now, sure." Following his gaze, I saw that the cattle had begun to drift before the storm, the night guards being evidently unable to cope with them, while at the other wagons, riders were saddling in hot haste and spurring off to their help through the blinding rain. Some of us at once ran out to our own saddle-band.

All of the ponies were standing huddled together, with their heads down and their tails to the wind. They were wild and restive enough usually; but the storm had cowed them, and we were able to catch them without either rope or halter. We made quick work of saddling; and the second each man was ready, away he loped through the dusk, splashing and slipping in the pools of water that studded the muddy plain. Most of the riders were already out when we arrived. The cattle were gathered in a compact, wedge-shaped, or rather fan-shaped mass, with their tails to the wind—that is, toward the thin end of the wedge or fan. In front of this fan-shaped mass of frightened, maddened beasts was a long line of cowboys, each muffled in his slicker and with his broad hat pulled down over his eyes, to shield him from the pelting rain. When the cattle were quiet for a moment, every horseman at once turned round with his back to the wind, and the whole line stood as motionless as so many sentries. Then, if the cattle began to spread out and overlap at the ends, or made a rush and broke through at one part of the lines, there would be a change into wild activity. The men, shouting and swaying in their saddles, darted to and fro with reckless speed, utterly heedless of danger—now racing to the threatened point, now checking and wheeling their horses so sharply as to bring them square on their haunches, or even throw them flat down, while the hoofs plowed long furrows in the slippery soil, until, after some minutes of this mad galloping hither and thither, the herd, having drifted a hundred yards or so, would be once more brought up standing. We always had to let them drift a little to prevent their spreading out too much. The din of the thunder was terrific, peal following peal until they mingled in one continuous, rumbling roar; and at every thunderclap louder than its fellows, the cattle would try to break away. Darkness had set in, but each flash of lightning showed us a dense array of tossing horns and staring eyes. It grew always harder to hold in the herd; but the drift took us along to the corrals already spoken of, whose entrances were luckily to windward. As soon as we reached the first, we cut off part of the herd and turned it within; and after again doing this with the second, we were able to put all the remaining animals into the third. The instant the cattle were housed, five-sixths of the horsemen started back at full speed for the wagons; the rest of us barely waited to put up the bars and make the corrals secure before galloping after them. We had to ride right in the teeth of the driving storm; and once at the wagons, we made small delay in crawling under our blankets, damp though the latter were, for we were ourselves far too wet, stiff, and cold not to hail with grateful welcome any kind of shelter from the wind and the rain.

All animals were benumbed by the violence of this gale of cold rain: a prairie chicken rose from under my horse's feet so heavily that, thoughtlessly striking at it, I cut it down with my whip; while when a jackrabbit got up ahead of us, it was barely able to limp clumsily out of our way.

But though there is much work and hardship, rough fare, monotony, and exposure connected with the roundup, yet there are few men who do not look forward to it and back to it with pleasure. The only fault to be found is that the hours of work are so long that one does not usually have enough time to sleep. The food, if rough, is good: beef, bread, pork, beans, coffee or tea, always canned tomatoes, and often rice, canned corn, or sauce made from dried apples. The men are good-humored, bold, and thoroughly interested in their business, continually vying with one another in the effort to see which can do the work best. It is superbly health-giving, and is full of excitement and adventure, calling for the exhibition of pluck, self-reliance, hardihood, and dashing horsemanship; and of all forms of physical labor, the easiest and pleasantest is to sit in the saddle.

CATTLE BRANDING

It is best to brand all the calves and mavericks on the same day, as afterward, the cattle are often turned loose to run on the same range on which they were caught. But if the outfit to which they belong has its principal range at some distance, the newly branded batch must be taken off and driven to their home range.

THE CORRAL

It is not absolutely necessary to have a corral to brand in, but if you can run your bunch into one, it saves trouble. The corral is roughly and strongly made of posts and rails, about five feet high. It ought to be large enough to hold your bunch of cattle and leave room for working. Just outside a fire is lit, and one man keeps the brands hot. He passes them through the rails as they are called for.

It is always better to arrange the corrals with pens and shoots for both separating the different brands and for doing the necessary cutting, branding, etc., but this is not always possible.

BRANDING CALVES

In a small corral, one man on horseback is enough inside, and even he can be dispensed with unless there are large calves to handle. A man with a rope catches a calf by throwing the loop over his head. If the calf is a little fellow, he is dragged to one side, caught, thrown down, cut, and branded in a very short time.

But a calf of even two or three months is not always easily managed. After the noose has been tightened on his neck, the end of the rope is then passed around one of the rails. The calf gallops up and down the arena at the fullest length of his tether, jumping and bellowing as if he knew his end was coming. By slow degrees the rope is overhauled, and the length that gives the calf play is shortened. One of the men will then go up to it, catching it by a noose around the neck in one hand, and passing his hand over its back, by the loose skin on its flank near the stifle, with the other.

The more the calf jumps, the better, but if he is slow and lethargic, the cowboy will often give him a shake to set him jumping. So, marking time with the prancing calf, the man seizes the animal as it leaves the ground, puts a knee under him to turn his body over, and then drops him on his side. Another man catches hold of a hind leg and stretches it out to its full length. The first man sits near the calf's head, with one knee on the neck, and doubles up one forefoot.

A good-sized calf can give a lot of trouble. After the rope around the neck has been drawn up, another noose is thrown to catch one of the hind legs, which should be the one not on the side to be branded. This rope is also passed around a rail, and is hauled tight till the animal is well extended. Somebody takes hold of his tail, and with a strong jerk, throws him onto his side. A hitch is taken with the same rope around his other hind foot and the noose is loosened around his throat, but the man leans his boot on the calf's neck and holds his foreleg tightly. He must look out for the animal's head, as the calf throws it about, and if it should strike the man's thigh instead of the ground, as it is very liable to do, the puncher will receive a bruise from the young horns, which he will not forget for a good many days.

The brand should not be red hot, and when applied to the hide, should be pressed only just enough to keep it in one place. The brand, if properly done, shows by a pink color that it has bitten into the skin, through the hair. Some of the stock, in the early spring, have very shaggy coats, and a brand that only marks the hair of their hide in most cases will leave a bad mark which would hardly show nextwinter.

The calves generally lie quietly and do not bellow, even when they feel the hot iron. But a few make up for the ones by roaring and bellowing to beat the band.

When the operation is finished, the calf generally gets up quietly, as soon as it feels the rope loosen, and rejoins the others.

The cows seldom interfere to protect their young, but when you do find one on the warpath, she makes the ring lively, and all hands need to be prepared, at short notice, to nimbly climb the fence or jump over.

To work steadily at catching, throwing, and branding is hard work. The sun is hot, the corral is full of dust from the cattle running round and round, and your jeans and shirt are soon spoiled with the blood and dirt of the operation. You may have, besides, taken a tumble yourself when throwing a calf. The process is still worse if rain has fallen, and the cattle have probably, for want of time the day they were corralled, been shut up through the night. As they run round and round to avoid the man they see swinging his loop, the whole area is churned into mud.

There is a lot of excitement about this business. The cowboys will work long hours. The boss is a happy fellow, and never tires, running backward and forward between the fire and the struggling calves. Each time he slaps on the brand, he seals a bit of property. He would like to work at this all day long. If the corral is very large the ropes are thrown by a man on horseback. As soon as a calf is caught, he takes a turn with the end of the rope around the horn of his saddle, and the horse drags the animal to the right spot.

A cow accustomed to men on horseback will sometimes run after her calf with her nose stretched down toward it. But when she nears the men on foot, the cow stops and leaves the calf to its fate.

If branding is done in the open, one man holds the bunch together, and the lassoer picks out the unbranded calves and drags them off to the fire.

BRANDING BIG COWS

Throwing big cattle does them no good.

If large cattle have to be branded, you cannot expect to do much without horses. The lasso should be thrown over the horns only, and three or four men are needed to hold the animal after it is down. When it comes to an old bull, and he declines to be manhandled, even a couple of ropes thrown over his horns and tied to a post are snapped like pack thread. In this case, he can be branded by a man on horseback with a hot iron in his hand, by following the bull into the thick of the herd. Jammed in the corner of the corral, the bull can move but slowly, and there is time to press the brand, and to leave a mark.

One man should be able to catch, throw, and brand a cow on the plain, but even with two or three men, this is not always accomplished very speedily. Sometimes, should one man dismount, the enraged cow makes for him. If the rope is held tight, there is no danger outside its reach, but sometimes the rope breaks, or in the charging and shifting, the man on foot may get between the animal and the horse. The cow will make a rush, and the man is lucky if he can escape a tumble and a kick.

BREAKING HORSES
TO SADDLE

Once the cattle have been rounded up, sorted, branded, and driven to the railhead for shipment east, or delivered for sale to the army post or abattoir, the remaining horses that have been rounded up are divided into separate bands according to their several ownerships. Each owner selects the animals to be sold, and also chooses a few likely animals suitable for training into cow ponies, to be used in the work of the ranch. Each of these specimens must be sound in body and quick footed. Well-trained cow ponies were regarded as aristocrats. They brought prices three times that of well-broken but more commonplace range horses. The term "pony" does not necessarily suggest diminutiveness, because the West gave the title of "pony" to almost every horse regardless of its size, and exempted from this class only "workhorses" and such brutes as by despicable viciousness merited the description of "that damned cayuse."

A horse that could travel notably far, particularly at high speed, was termed a "long horse." Consequently, the best stayer in one's band would be called one's "longest horse." There was no such phrase as "long pony," though any given animal might be both a "cow pony" and a "long horse."

The pony might be particularly good at cutting out, a fast runner in a spurt, but a bit shy of a thrown lariat, or not an expert in doing its part after the reata had made its catch. Nevertheless, he might be invaluable in driving stock, despite his restricted usefulness in the game played in the corral. Another pony, perfect at the roping work, might be slow in a dash to head stock running in the open; but notwithstanding this, he might be just right for the work within the corral. Some ponies did all things well, and they were regarded as being of almost royal rank.

As a result of this lack of uniformity in the horses' qualifications, cowboys were often assigned several ponies, one animal for one class of work, another for another. Often a cowboy was also assigned a horse of less attainment, to be used in the commonplace tasks and errands of the everyday. The various animals assigned to a man were left strictly alone by all other men on the ranch; and the horses' assignee, so long as he rode for the ranch, was sole lord of, and responsible for, his string.

After a rough and hurried "gentling" of the inferior horses at the rodeo corral—these horses were to be sold off to some none-too-discerning buyer and needed to be put through at least the rudiments of breaking—the punchers delivered them to their destination, and then drove the remaining animals to the corrals at the ranch house. In and around these home corrals, each of the horses that were to be kept as cow ponies—or were to be sold as truly "gentled" animals—would be selected and during the ensuing months, would be more or less carefully broken.

The reason for the earlier hurried "gentling" at the rodeo, or roundup corral was that nobody seriously cared whether these second-rate animals were spoiled or not. So the punchers, both local and visiting, made something of a lark of the whole business and reverted to the active use of quirt and spur.

"GENTLING" AT THE RANCH

But the work at the ranch was a different matter and there was not much recourse to the spur and quirt because the horses gentled there represented the best quality that the ranch could boast, and were not to be jeopardized. There, grown horses in process of breaking were thrown by the lariat only when necessity demanded. Instead, with their necks through the reata's loop, they pranced about at end of a rope like kites in a storm. As this circling continued, the reata was gradually gathered in, and the cowboy soon found himself holding a rope of controlling length within handling distance of the captive.

Next the hackamore was shown to the trembling animal and was placed on his head, to rest there a half hour or so. Perhaps that same day, a similar exhibition was made of the saddle. It was placed as gently as possible on the twitching back, and the cinches, after being circumspectly and successfully fished, were quietly made fast. A long, crooked stick was most convenient for this fishing operation, because at times the air was quite full of hoofs.

After the horse had become accustomed to the feeling of the hackamore and saddle—it might be for a matter of minutes and a single saddling, or of a day or two and repeated saddling—a rider mounted him. Later the horse was similarly introduced to the bit.

The reason for this quasi-tenderness was that the object of most ranchmen was not to make horses buck, but to keep them from doing so. The cowboy was hired, so far as concerned horses, not to encourage but to discourage pitching. He was paid to turn unbroken horseflesh into money, and the ordinary buyer will not exchange his dollars for useless, vertical motion. Hence, one ordinarily saw at a well-managed ranch only the bucking that could not be avoided. Instead there was much effort to wean a horse from this habit. There were, of course, exceptions, but the number of "rough riding" men was comparatively small.

The above account of breaking horses sets forth the method employed by the majority of the ranchers after the first years of the Kingdom of Cattle, when "busting wide open" by "quirting a plenty," and "shoving in the steel," were the accepted means of gentling, though it should be remembered that the later ranchers dealt principally with the "graded horse" while the earlier stockmen had little but the unmixed wild horse to work with.

ROUGH RIDING

The rough rider's object was to "break the pony's heart" on the first riding; this was concluded because, if the idea of human supremacy could be impressed upon a physically exhausted animal, then it was relatively certain that the pony would never again make that violent of an effort. True, it might buck again, but never so fiercely. The latent dread of man would cloud every subsequent inclination to pitch. To create this dread, the rough-riding buster brought down the quirt at every jump the pony made.

These rough riders usually were either owners of small ranches, or else were men who, as itinerant "contract busters," went from ranch to ranch and temporarily leased their services to those who could not afford to maintain a first-class rider of their own. These busters might receive five dollars for each animal they "busted," "broke," "peeled," "twisted," or "gentled."

Their method was to intimidate, first, by roping and violently throwing the animal, next and as soon as the saddle was in position, by wholesale use of the quirt, a lashing which on occasion was augmented by the whips and howls of assistant terrorists, sometimes called "hazers." When the men's arms grew tired and it was agreed that the pony was in chastened mood, the buster mounted; and if the welted animal again began to pitch, the quirting commenced anew.

The buster might do the initial riding with one of the crueler sorts of bit, but he was more apt at first to use a "hackamore" and to reserve the bit for a later lesson.

The buster frequently extended the lesson beyond the time that he himself was in the saddle. After dismounting, he was apt to place a hackamore on the pony's head, and to fasten its reins to the end of a long rope tied to a peg driven in the ground, thus to the end of a stake or picket-rope. With or without encouragement from the hazers, the fastened horse was likely to run to the end of his tether, to have his wind suddenly cut by the tightening hackamore, and at the rope's end, to somersault onto his back. This action might be repeated several times before the animal desisted.

By plenteous quirting and the stake rope's aid, the buster endeavored to inculcate "fear of leather," and a dread of "running against rope."

If the gentled animal were to be sold to strangers, two days of this rough treatment might suffice to satisfy the conscience of the ranch, but if the beast were to be used at home, it would receive a week of training and abuse.

The intelligent, orderly method which is first above described, and which did not avoid finesse though it attempted to abolish cruelty, should not be confused with the affectionate, misguided, and desultory schooling occasionally employed by amateurs and productive of one of the meanest, most unreliable objects in the Cattle Country—a "pet horse."

Although the decent method of breaking was far more gentle than was the "buster's" riot with the steel and quirt, its relative softness did not wholly free the bronco from the lash and rowel, or rob him of a wholesome respect for the possibilities of "leather." A pony, once thrown, never thereafter outgrew the recollection of the lariat's spilling ability. This doubtless explains why "gentled" horses, however mean, were often securely corralled by an enclosure made of no more than a single line of rope held withers high called a *remuda*.

At the roundup, in camp, anywhere, lariats were tied end to end, and were stretched along a line of nondescript posts which might be wholly or in part trees, men, wagon-wheels, or the horns of saddles atop sedate old nags. A band of saddleless riding horses would arrive upon the gallop, and at sight of that one strand of rope, would stop short to stand there and await the saddle. This effective though very loose corral needed not to have even three enclosed sides. A wide-open V shape was an efficient form. Even a straight line would do. It was the compelling fear of the reata that held the animals. And yet a short time before, when as yet unintroduced to leather, they had rocked the sides of a log enclosure.

There was less of equine violence during the "gentling" process than might be expected, for usually the animals were ridden by competent horsemen. The cow pony was a better judge of the rider's ability than any riding-master. Just put your foot in a stirrup, and in an instant you have been accurately appraised by the horse you have mounted; and broadly speaking, no western steed, so long as he remained physically sound, was so craven as to tolerate an incompetent horseman on his back for long.

Horse breaking, when actually done by competent horsemen, produced averages recorded as follows:

Practically every horse, at its first saddling when it was on the leash of a hackamore and before any attempt was made to mount the brute, "bucked the saddle." If the horse was not abused at this stage of training, and while held by the hackamore or by a lariat about its neck, was cajoled, in eighty cases out of one hundred, it quieted down, and eventually, on the same day or else at the second saddling on the day after, tremblingly, hesitatingly, permitted itself to be mounted by a competent horseman, without offering to buck the rider.

A few of these pious eighty might "crowhop" for a while— that is, jump about with arched back and stiffened knees—but this is not true bucking.

There were left from the hundred animals, twenty that would buck more or less at their first riding, ten of which would continue to buck more or less at their second or even third riding, but only two of which could be counted on to remain permanent pitchers.

Of these two, one could be so well broken that it would "go after" its rider only when a long rest at pasture had lessened recollection of human supremacy. The other, though rideable, would buck whenever it became excited or irritated.

One horse in approximately each five hundred was an "outlaw," a brute that never could be broken and that would buck almost in its sleep.

MAN KILLERS

One horse, it is supposed, in approximately each ten thousand was sufficiently a "man-killer" as to deliberately jump on his thrown rider's prostrate body. The actual man-killer—traditionally always a male—was a horse so rare that the average ranchman in his whole working life saw not more than one. The beast was a devil masquerading in the body of a horse, a devil that, at sight of man, cunningly planned to kill him.

Ensconced amid the stock placidly feeding on the range, the brute would sight an approaching horseman or pedestrian, would gently disengage itself from its fellows, would trot quietly forward as though mild and friendly curiosity were its only incentive, and then suddenly and without warning, would spring ahead in a frenzied rage and strike down the man, together with the saddle-animal under him.

If mixed in a swiftly moving roundup, it had no opportunity thus to stalk its prey, it would bide its time, and would, in apparent innocence, hasten along with the driven band, meanwhile edging toward the intended victim. When the moment for attack arrived, the brute would wheel, and with hard-set face, open mouth, and glittering eye would come on like a destroying demon. While the man-killer at times would kill riderless horses, either in the corral or out upon the range, the favorite prey was the human being.

Although, during its peaceful moods, men usually could not distinguish it from a normal animal, ridden horses frequently diagnosed it from afar. Because mounts tended to quiver and swerve in the midst of loose horses, it became traditional among riders that the "six gun" should be drawn at once. "Kill him, the second he shows he's one, or he'll get you sure," was the slogan of the ranchmen.

The pedestrian on the open range did run a danger from man-killing horses. That danger, however, was so slight as to be almost academic. But he was at constant risk from all cattle, especially from the cows. For a dismounted man, the range cow was, under average conditions, a far more dangerous adversary than was the grizzly bear. Under those average conditions, the cow would always attack, while the bear would almost always avoid a conflict.

A man on foot would be far out in the grass. A cow amid a bunch of cattle would spy him and start toward him. The others would follow. The bunch, starting at a walk, would presently break into a trot, and finally would begin to move in a spiral about the victim. So far, inquisitiveness apparently had been the only stimulus. Suddenly "tails would roll," and with savage fury, the herd would quicken to a gallop and sweep over the helpless victim. Hoofs would crush out his life.

Men had, of course, to work afoot at the branding fires, and sometimes within the corrals; but these men were guarded by watchful horsemen with ready lariats. It was never a good idea to stay alone and afoot within a corral containing cattle.

Scattered about the West were "spoiled horses," animals that man, by kicks in the face or by other abuse during the breaking period, had ruined as to character, and which, engraved on their hearts the motto, "No one shall ever stay on our backs" held throughout their lives as closely as they could to their resolve and bucked and bucked and bucked. They were merely manmade "outlaws."

BUCKING AND PITCHING

Between "bucking" and "pitching," there is little difference except that of geography. The northwesterner called it "bucking" or "buck jumping." The Texan called the Texan it was "pitching."

Bucking itself needs little description. Every one who is familiar with its component motions can well imagine *straight bucking, sun fishing*, the *end for end*, and the *back throw*.

A horse is said to be doing *straight work* when he keeps his body headed in one general direction, however high he might arch his back one moment, however sway-backed he might be the instant afterward. He might land over and over on the same spot, or he might *pitch a plungin'*, also called a *running buck* or *bucking straight away*; in other words: jump forward with each buck.

An ingenious pony might embellish this straight work by giving it a seesaw effect—that is landing alternately on his front and hind legs, or else by bucking not in the vertical plane but diagonally upward, and leaning first to the right and then to the left. He might also vary the motion with snakelike contortions of his spine, by shakes and shivers, by rearward jumps, and by sudden downward and sideway shimmies of shoulder or hip.

He might leave the ground headed at one compass point and land headed at another. If so, then he is said to be *pitchin' fence-cornered*.

If he twists his body into a crescent, he qualifies as *sun fishin'*, and if in producing this motion, he merges it into an exaggerated *fence-cornering*, going up headed, say, northeast and landing headed, say, northwest, he takes the prize.

He might substitute straight north and south for these directions, and is then said to be bucking *end for end* or *swapping ends.*

Bucking might be terminated by a *rear back*, or *back fall*, sometimes by a *back throw*, sometimes by a *side throw*, or on very rare occasions by a *pinwheel*. Usually it is ended by the failure of the tired bronco to buck any longer.

The difference between the *rear back*, or *back fall*, and the *back throw*, is one of speed and motive. In the *rear back*, or *back fall*—depending on what you call it—the horse, attempting to stand erect upon its hind legs, quivers, unintentionally loses its balance, and falls. In the *back throw*, he purposely overrears and hurls himself backward onto the ground.

The *pinwheel* sends the horse—or cow—on a forward and upward jump, to turn feet up in the air and to land on its back. Most fortunately, it is extremely seldom that an animal achieves this movement.

The direction of the *side throw* is suggested by its name.

Such were the outstanding, technical expressions that earmarked the various specialties in pitching. Modern days have filched terms from modern sources and applied them—in a slangy sense—to modern buckers. At present-day rodeos you hear of horses "aviating," doing "nosedives," "high dives," or "tailspins," being "skyscrapers," having "six cylinders," and "skipping on two of them," "stepping on the gas," doing the "cakewalk," being the "best pitcher in the league," being a "side winder," and "good thrower to second base." But such phrases are creations of the present and were unknown on the open range of bygone years.

Every rider of a horse that acts viciously is on the watch for kicks and bites, and keeps himself on the lookout for the dreaded **rear back**, **back throw**, or less dangerous **side throw**, but can pretty much dismiss the **pinwheel** from the list of prospective probabilities. There's no percentage in worrying about it. There is no escape from the pinwheel, and no method of preventing it.

Some animals, planning to unseat their riders, at the instant of mounting, resort not to the buck, but to the more prosaic strategy of simply running away, or of calmly lying down. Such a prone horse is very likely to receive some uncomfortable treatment, for his rider, now standing over him, might with steady, upward pull on the reins keep the pony's head up off the ground, and with one foot pressing steadily down on the saddle horn, the horse is deprived of the leverage of its neck, the balance weight of its head, and consequently of any ability to roll its body or to regain its feet. When the pony's neck has received sufficient cramping, he usually will offer to rise, and as he reaches his feet, the cowboy is once again in the saddle.

Or else the rider simply kept his feet in the stirrups, one of his legs remaining under the lying-down horse, relying on the lightness of the horse, the softness of the ground, the strength of his stirrup, and the thickness of his chaps for the safety of his leg. He also trusted that some bystander would rope and hold the feet of the animal, should it attempt to roll. When the horse became tired of this prone position, it would lurch to its feet and have the man still aboard. Some riders strive to stick to their mount no matter what. They believe that quitting the saddle will give the horse undue confidence, and will retard if not annul his growing belief in the supremacy of man. All the time that the horse was lying prone, the rider would talk to him in soothing tones. And throughout bucking, the rider and the pony are likely to enter into a kind of game of call and response. The sound of the human voice is thought to be one means of proving to the horse that he had met his master. The unhappy animal whinnies, snorts, and pitches, the rider answering each throw firmly, and with some profanity.

The man atop a runaway is usually willing to let the beast "run down its mainspring," but he might promptly stop the animal if he didn't mind jeopardizing his own neck. If this man were to reach forward and grasp either the rein or the bridle at a point close to the bit, and just as the horse is lifting its front feet, were to pull the pony's head sharply to one side, the animal would fall on its flank on the ground. A less dangerous method is to lean forward and put a handkerchief, hat, or some other blind over the eyes of the runaway. This will pretty much stop him in his tracks.

There are, broadly speaking, two methods of riding the buck. One as to *sit it* or, to *ride straight up*; that is, to sit

upright and squarely in the saddle, shifting one's balance with every change in the horse's position.

If the man sitting the buck is a good rider, he keeps his seat and his legs so closely to the saddle as never to bounce upward, and thus, even for an instant, to **show daylight** beneath his body.

Less accomplished riders **hunt leather**, **take leather**, **touch leather**, **pull leather,** or **go to leather**, as a handhold on any part of the saddle, its accoutrements, or the horse was interchangeably known. He might **choke the horn**, or **choke**, or **squeeze the biscuit**, as a handhold on the saddle horn was called. But not so the jaunty top rider. He scorned such aid, and never locked his spurs or tied his stirrups. He **rode slick**. The other method of riding the buck involves the rider seizing the horn in one or both hands, his pushing himself sideways out of the saddle and standing in one stirrup, with his knee on that side flexed, and his other leg at its midway point between hip and knee resting horizontally across the saddle's seat. His flexed knee joint and his two hip joints collectively absorbed the shock.

RODEO RIDING

In a rodeo or other formal riding competitions, anyone who—competing in a class reserved for top riders and in which **hunting leather** is barred—gives even an accidental, momentary, slight touch of any part of either hand to any portion of the saddle after mounting had been completed, receives a demerit for each offense, or depending on the rules, is at once disqualified.

Indifferent horsemen, more fearful of pitching than of the taunting tongues of onlookers, used to tie, or hobble their stirrups; in other words to connect them by a strap or rope passing under the horse. This had the advantage of offering a firm anchorage during bucking, but had the disadvantage of imposing a social stigma, as bystanders were wont to insist that no real horseman would do such a thing.

Occasionally some daredevil puncher rode with *slick heels*—without spurs, or else rode a horse, a mule, or a steer either bareback or with only a cinch or lariat around the animal's body. All these, however, are exhibition stunts, and are no part of ranching work.

The "gentling" of the horses gathered at the roundup was eventually finished. At last came the time to ship, and the punchers headed toward the railway with their charges. The expedition traveled by day and rested at night in the same manner as though the men were driving cattle. But it moved more rapidly, and there was much less fear of possible stampede, though a horse stampede once started was far more difficult to stop than was the "bust up" of a cattle herd.

MONTANA

NORTH DAKOTA

Bozeman

Miles City

SOUTH DAKOTA

Deadwood
Rapid City

WYOMING

Fort Laramie

NEBRASKA

Cheyenne

Ogallala

Fort Morgan

COLORADO

KANSAS

Denver

Kit Carson

Ellsworth

Abilene

Kansas City

Sedalia

St. Louis

Pueblo

Trail City

Dodge City

Newton

Wichita

MISSOURI

NATIONAL TRAIL

Camp Supply

Boone's Springs

NEW MEXICO

OKLAHOMA

Fort Gibson

Fort Summer

Fort Sill

Doan's Store

Fort Smith

ARKANSAS

Red River Station

TEXAS

Fort Griffin

Fort Worth

Fort Concho

Horsehead Crossing

Waco

Uvalde

San Antonio

HISTORIC
CATTLE TRAILS
NORTH FROM TEXAS

SCALE OF MILES
0   50   100   150   200   250

THE CATTLE DRIVE, OR TRAILING THE HERD

"We started north with the grass. Had thirty-three hundred head of twos and threes, with a fair string of saddle stock."

—Andy Adams

Once the roundup was completed, the aim was to drive, or *trail* the herd to a shipping point—usually a railhead—or if the animals were to be sold to the government, an army post or fort. Horses were a different matter, because the terms of their sale might require that they be well broken—or at least somewhat *gentled*—so they were taken instead to the corrals of the owner's home ranch.

Each outfit organized itself differently, depending on the size of herd, the conditions and length of the route, and the vagaries of the particular owner of the herd, but generally the outfit consisted of a foreman or *trail boss*, his assistant or (from the Spanish) *segundo*, and the cook. The number of hands varied, but a good rule of thumb put their number at something like one cowboy for each 250 cattle. Oddly enough, a large herd was controlled more easily than was a small one.

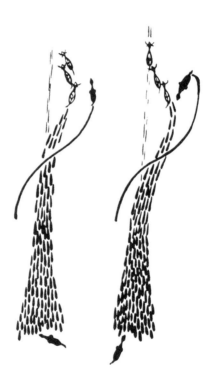

No puncher rode directly in front of the column. The theory was that the less the herd realized that it was under check, the more disposed it would be to behave itself. Nevertheless, on each side of the column, parallel with it, and at a little distance from it rode a line of cowboys with long intervals between the men. The foremost of the punchers in each of these lines rode slightly ahead of the herd and was called a *point man* or *head rider*. Each of the men in line behind him was called a *swing man* or *flank rider*. At the rear of the column came the *tail riders*. Bringing up the rear was the herd of horses the cowboys used as remounts or the *remuda*—bossed by the *wrangler*, and finally the chuck wagon.

The function of the *swing men* was to block their own cattle from any sidewise wandering or tendency to go walkabout, and also to fend off any foreign cattle that might try to merge themselves into the herd.

For the first week, the herd was "shoved along" at a quite reasonable speed, the idea being that the stock would tire into submissiveness, and afterward willingly keep to the course that their owners intended. During that week considerable mileage was made, though not always in one direction, but eventually the herd settled down and would make a daily progress of ten or fifteen miles, depending on the character of the terrain.

The whole operation started each morning at sunup, crawled on till late afternoon, and then, as a preliminary to halting for the night and as a preventive of entanglement with other traveling herds, was "thrown off" a half mile or more from the side of the trail. For the halting place, the so-called *bed ground*, the cowboys, in order to satisfy the cattle's inborn preferences, did heir best to find land that offered fresh grass to eat, old, dry grass to lie on, and if the weather were warm, an elevation sufficient to catch a breeze.

NIGHT HERD

Throughout their daylong march, the animals nibbled the grass they passed, but at evening they set themselves to a solid meal. This eaten, the cattle pursued, as did range horses, the same regimen as of most wild animals. Two hours after dark, they one by one sank down to sleep. At midnight they rose again to browse for a couple of hours, then back to sleep for an hour or so, then another browsing followed by another nap until dawn. But if the moon was full, they were likely to browse all night long.

All through the hours of darkness, the men of the *night herd*, working in shifts of from two to four hours, rode around the animals; and as they rode they often serenaded the cattle by crooning to them. This serenading was done partly to hold the cattle under the compelling spell of the human voice, and partly to disabuse from the mind of any fearful member of the herd suspicion that a cowboy's silhouette against the sky or the noise of his moving pony might represent danger.

The rider, when "singing the cattle," as his vocal efforts were sometimes styled, sang all the words he knew, set to all the tunes he could remember or invent, but carefully omitted any sound or inflection which might startle. Church hymns were usual, because their simple melodies were easily

remembered. But the words set to these sacred airs might well have surprised the clergy. Besides the proper words, these songs might also include accounts of horse races, unflattering opinions of the cattle, strings of profanity, the text remembered from the labels of coffee cans or vegetable tins. Mere humming sounds also were chanted with deep religious fervor, and on many a night were poured into the appreciative ears of the cloven-hoofed audience.

Thus tired men, catnapping but always crooning, were out in the night, their ponies steadily, slowly patrolling, though half-asleep; but man and horse were ready to wake like a shot and to act the instant that a steer started to "roll his tail," a sure sign of trouble.

STAMPEDE

Throughout the journey the animals had proceeded quietly and rested decently until one moment when with a snort, a bellow, and a chorus of lowing, everything changed. What caused this nobody knew or could stop to check, but "tails" had "rolled," and a stampede was on. Everywhere cattle began to move, lunging outward from the center of the herd and darting toward every point of the compass.

Every cowboy leaped for his saddle, and armed with blankets, hats, and even plucked sagebrush—anything that could be waved—galloped out beyond the panicked and fleeing cattle. The trick was to head and to flank them, and eventually get them all moving in the same direction. The riders on the flanks now sought to soothe and slow the herd,

while the man or men on the point worked to turn the head of the herd in on itself and thus bring it more or less to a halt. Then followed a period of **milling**, as the unhappy animals moved about within the herd grunting and lowing, surrounded in clouds of choking dust—or if a thunderstorm had been the cause of the melee—in pelting rain.

The riders were luck if they had come through without serious injury—or worse. It had been a dangerous game.

Eventually the milling stopped, and the animals began to graze.

After every stampede the cattle were counted, and punchers tasked to hunt down the absentees and cut out the stray animals that become swept up into the herd during the progress of the stampede.

CUTTING THE TRAIL

From time to time a **trail-cutter** might "cut the trail," which is to say might require the punchers to halt a moving herd, to permit an inspection, and to cut from the herd and deliver to the trail-cutter the animals, if any, as he was entitled to demand.

This cutting upon the drive was called "trimming the herd."

Any ranch owner whose range was traversed by the driven cattle had the right to cut the trail, and might do so in person or through any duly accredited employee. Such a trail-cutter

might demand from the drovers only the animals belonging
to the cutter's ranch. Each official stock inspector and range
detective might also cut the trail, and might demand all
animals which, though actually within the herd, did not legally
belong to it.

WATERING THE HERD

The routes usually chosen for the drive across the plains may be said to furnish, on an average, water every fifteen miles. In some instances, and during the hot season of the year, it is necessary in places to go into what was called "a dry camp"—that is, to encamp where there is no water. In such emergencies, with a previous knowledge of the route, it is a good idea to transport a sufficient quantity from the last camp to satisfy the needs of the hands, but the dumb brutes must make do with the little moisture obtained from the night grazing to quench their thirst.

Because of the sustained effort and the awful dust, both the cattle and the horses in driven herds required more frequent drink than when the animals were shifting for themselves. In addition, the farther they were "bred away" from the original "wild" blood, the more often they demanded water. During a drought wild horses and wild cattle would wander about for days without drinking, and could survive even though thirst might swell and blacken their tongues.

When loose on the range, horses and cattle needed access to water at least once every forty-eight hours; but if called upon to do so, could withstand thirst for a number of successive days. Many of them, for reasons known only to themselves, selected for their habitual grazing-grounds tracts far from any waterhole, and so regularly had to travel miles to and from their drinking spot.

Sometimes the punchers, on leaving one river, deliberately prevented their animals from drinking their fill in order that a lust for water might hold these animals through the semiarid desert that lay before the next river.

SWIMMING THE HERD

There is also the tricky business of swimming the herd across a swollen river or stream.

Hundreds of driven cattle are walking in a column perhaps a mile in length like scattered leaves blown across a lawn. Once they reach the stream's bank, singly or in pairs, the forward animals break out and lumber down the bank, trotting across the sandbar at and finally stand midknee in the water, their muzzles immersed.

The cowboys select one or two steers that promise courage and qualities of leadership, and quietly take up a position behind them, and as they raised their heads, urge them farther into the stream, into swimming water; and by heading all attempts to deviate from the course, get them to the opposite shore. A few adventurous cattle follow the leaders; and once all of these pioneers are across, the herd automatically passes down the bank, into the water, and across it.

"Starting the swim" was an anxious task, for if the selected leaders were to outwit the men and succeed in doubling back before leaving the shore or after entering the water, it might bring on a stampede—the steadily arriving cattle, on reaching the water's edge, swerving away from it and pursuing the animals ahead that have already turned and might now be galloping inland; or else a milling and interweaving jam of nervous animals steadily mushrooming from the forward pressure of the arriving animals, and ready at any moment to split and stampede.

As soon as the continuity of movement was assured, a cowboy or two plunged their horses into the water, made their way to the opposite shore, and set about clearing it of its clogging cattle and getting them into marching order on the plain beyond.

Some of the men, preferring stability to comfort, made no change in their riding position while in the water, and swimming wet, landed with clothing dripping between knee and hip. Others, more finical, bent their knees and raised their feet, with their spurs touching the cantle. A rider of this type ran the risk of being unbalanced by an unexpected eddy or a bumping steer, and rolling his top-heavily burdened horse directly on its side; or else, through instinctive and unfortunate pull on the reins, of rearing his horse, only to have it madly splash its front legs and then flop sideways. A successful grab of a stirrup, or better still, of a tail's end might give this hapless rider an efficient tow to safety.

The men's familiarity with this crossing, as well as the act of traversing it, relieved them from any anxiety about possible quicksand. If the ford was unfamiliar to the trail boss, he would see that both banks were well scouted before he attempted to take his herd across. The treacherous sands of many a western stream have swallowed many a horse and steer. The only remedy for quicksand is a lariat and a tugging pony

If milling had begun in earnest in the stream, mounted punchers and the ponies under them did their best to struggle through the whirling mess, to break its motion, to resolve its participants into line, and to connect that line's front end with the desired shore. A pony might be crushed, might have his trappings entangled in the horns of a sinking steer. A rider might meet with a similar catastrophe. Yet for the punchers, the worst that usually befell a man breaking a mill was to be tossed from his mount and to go ashore on a steer's back or holding the end of its tail.

THE END OF THE TRAIL

At the end of lengthy cattle drives—notably that of the Texas trail—the cowboys, rebounding from the protracted, grueling duties, were prone to "let off a little steam." Dodge City, Abilene, Newton, and their sister cow towns standing at the end of the long trail were seen, for the dusty, tired, jubilant, arriving puncher, as places of frolic and of license.

Morality with many a man is local. He might refuse to foul
his own nest; but when traveling far away from it, his sense
of decorum and decency is apt to decrease in proportion to
the square of the distance. As one old cowpoke said, "Many a
virtuous polar bear raises hell on the equator."

84

THE COWBOY GETUP

"They paid us off, and I bought some new clothes and got my picture taken. I had a new white Stetson hat that I paid ten dollars for and new pants that cost twelve dollars, and a good shirt and fancy boots. Lord was I proud of those clothes! When my sister saw me she said: 'Take your pants out of your boots and put your coat on. You look like an outlaw.' I told her to go to hell. And I never did like her after that."

—Teddy Blue Abbott

The clothing worn by cowboys was distinctive, and although picturesque, it was worn, not for effect, but solely because it was the dress best suited to the work at hand. Inasmuch as it was selected with a view only to comfort and convenience, it knew nothing of variable fashion and suffered little change in style.

It, however, was subject, as were many of the cowboys' customs, to differences according to locality, as was the line of demarcation between Northwest and the Southwest, and though never very clearly defined, it was in effect an imaginary westward extension of Mason and Dixon Line—this extension zigzagging a bit in some places.

HAT

The hat was usually of smooth, soft felt; and in color, dove gray, less often light brown, occasionally black. It had a cylindrical crown seven inches or more in height, and a flat brim so wide as to overtop its wearer's shoulders. The brim might or might not be edged with braid, which, if so, was silken and of the same color as the felt. In the Southwest, the crown was left at its full height, but its circumference above the summit of the wearer's head was contracted by three or, more commonly, four, vertical, equidistant dents, resembling a mountain whose sharp peak descended three or four deep gullies. In the Northwest, the crown was left flat on top, but was so far telescoped by a pleat as to remain but approximately two and a half inches high.

Few men of either section creased their hats in the manner of the other. A denizen of the Northwest appearing in a high-crowned hat was thought to be putting on airs, and was likely to be accused of "chucking the Rio," which was vernacular for aping the manners of the southwesterners, whose chief river was the Rio Grande.

Around the crown, just above the brim and for the purpose of regulating the fit of the hat, ran a belt, which was adjustable as to length. The belt was usually made of leather, but particularly in the Southwest, occasionally of woven silver or gold wire. The belt, if of leather, was often studded with ornamental nails—or if the owner's purse permitted—with **conchas**, which were flat metal plates, usually circular, generally of silver. For the leather itself, some men would substitute the skin of a rattlesnake.

From both sides of the brim at its inner edge, hung a buckskin thong; these two thongs, sometimes called "bonnet strings," which tied together and so formed a guard, which, during rapid riding or in windy weather, was tucked behind under the base of the skull or under the chin, but which at other times was simply thrust inside the hat.

The wide brim of the hat was not for appearance's sake. It was for use. It defended the cowboy from a burning sun and shaded his eyes when clearness of vision was vital to a man awake or shelter was desirable for one asleep. In rainy weather it served as an umbrella. The brim, when grasped between the thumb and fingers and bent into a trough, was the only their drinking-cup outdoors; and when pulled down and tied over the ears, it gave real protection from frostbite. It fanned every campfire into activity, and enlarged the carrying capacity of the hat when used as a pail to transport water for extinguishing embers. This broad hat, swung to the right or left of the body, or overhead provided conspicuous means of signaling; and when shoved between one's hip or shoulder and the hard ground, it sometimes hastened the arrival of a nap. Folded, it made a comfortable pillow. No narrow-brimmed creation could have served so many functions.

A Philadelphian manufacturer virtually monopolized the making of at least the better grades; and, from his name, every broad-brimmed head covering was apt to be designated as a "Stetson," instead of by either one of its two legitimate titles of "hat" and "somberos." While these two legitimate titles were interchangeable throughout the West, the Northwest leaned toward "hat," and the Southwest toward "sombrero."

There were other slang names, but none that had more than infrequent usage.

They included "lid," "war-bonnet," "conk cover," "hair case," and a host of similar inventions.

Southwesterners often wore the real sombrero of Mexico, with its high crown, either conical or cylindrical, its saucer-shaped brim, and its shaggy surface of plush, frequently embroidered with gold or silver thread. No northwesterner dared, while in his home country, to "chuck the Rio" to the extent of such headgear.

Most of these sombreros, though reaching the American wearer by the route of importation from Mexico, had been made in Philadelphia by the very manufacturer mentioned above.

Along the Southern border, some men, principally Mexicans, wore the huge straw hats of Mexico; but these generally were avoided by North Americans.

Many punchers had such vanity as to their hats that the makers gave, in the so-called "feather-weight" quality, a felt far better than that used in the shapes offered to city folk, and so fine as to roll up almost as would a handkerchief, a felt so costly that only ranchmen would pay its price. Not infrequently a puncher spent from two to six months' wages for his hat or sombrero and its ornamental belt.

HANDKERCHIEF

The handkerchief, which encircled every cowboy's neck, was intended as a mask for occasional use, and not as an article of dress. This handkerchief, diagonally folded and with its two thus most widely separated corners fastened together by a square knot, ordinarily hung loosely about the base of the wearer's neck, and as the cowpoke rode in behind a bunch of moving stock, the still knotted handkerchief's broadest part was pulled up over the wearer's mouth and nose. This mask eliminated the otherwise suffocating dust and made breathing possible, though it offered relatively like protection against stinging sleet and freezing wind.

The cowboy did not care to risk being without this very necessary mask when he should have need of it, and so he always kept it on the safest peg he knew—under his chin.

In color and material the handkerchief, though sometimes of silk, usually was of red bandanna cotton. It was red, not because the puncher specifically demanded it, but because that was the only color other than white ordinarily obtainable from the local shopkeepers. The shopping cowboy was usually tolerant except in his selection of hats, chaps, spurs, guns, ropes, and saddles.

The handkerchief-selling shopkeeper, in his own turn, had followed the line of least resistance; and being subject to no special demand for green, blue, or whatever, hadn't bothered to make a hunt for varied colors among the manufacturers and had stocked the article which he could most readily obtain, the red bandanna.

White handkerchiefs were eschewed by many punchers, because these handkerchiefs, when clean, reflected light; and thus sometimes, on the Range, called attention to their wearers when they wished to avoid notice by other people or by animals. Moreover, white too soon so suffered from sweat and dust.

SHIRT

There was nothing peculiar about the shirt beyond that it was always of cotton or wool, was usually collarless, and though of any checked, striped design, or solid color, almost never was red. That color was believed to disturb the cattle, and in any event, belonged to the miners. Furthermore, the puncher's taste in colors was in the main quite subdued.

Collars were pretty much unknown. On the whole, collars were sold separately from shirts. And a white one, starched, would have probably embarrassed the working cowpoke. But that did not keep the professional gamblers from wearing it. A "turn-down" collar of celluloid (of paper in the early years), would have made the gambler showily immaculate, and so would advertise his apparent prosperity.

Each of the cowboy's shirtsleeves was customarily drawn in above the elbow by a garter, which was of twisted wire or of elastic webbing, and often as an exception to the general demureness of sartorial tone, was brightly colored. Crude shades of pink or blue were much in favor.

JACKET, VEST, AND PANTS

Nor was there anything distinctive about the cowboy's jacket and trousers, which were woolen and in cut, of the sack-suit variety. However, the cowboy sometimes substituted for his woolen jacket one of similar cut, but made of either brown canvas or black or brown leather.

Denim overalls were considered beneath the dignity of riders, and were left to wearing by the farmers, the townsfolk, and the subordinate employees of the ranches.

The puncher's trousers, universally called "pants," stayed in place largely through luck, because the puncher both avoided *galluses,* the suspenders of the tenderfoot, as tending to bind the shoulders, and was also wary of supporting belts, as they, if drawn at all tightly, threatened hernia when one's horse was pitching. However, if the puncher were of Mexican blood, he might gird himself with a sash of red or green silk.

The pistol's belt, wide and looped for extra cartridges, usually sagged loosely, and so threw the weapon's weight upon the thigh instead of placing the strain on the abdomen.

Whenever possible the cowboy went coatless, but he always wore a vest. The coat tended to arrest his motion, also its wearing invited perspiration, and perspiration for a man destined to remain out of doors day and night in a country of cold winds was uncomfortable, if not dangerous.

In everyday life the vest was of an ordinary, civilian type, and usually was left unbuttoned. It was worn, not so much as a piece of clothing, but solely because its outside pockets gave handy storage, not only to matches but also to "makings," which last-mentioned articles were cigarette papers and a bag of "Bull Durham" tobacco.

The matches in the cowboy's pocket, like all matches on the range, came in thin sheets like coarsely toothed combs. They had small brown or blue heads that were slow to blaze up, and for some time after striking, merely bubbled, emitting strong sulfurous fumes. To light one, the cowboy tightened his trousers by raising his right knee, and then drew the match across the trousers' seat.

OVERCOAT

His overcoat or *duster* was of canvas, light brown in color, with skirts to the knee. It was blanket-lined, and to make it wholly wind-proof, commonly received an exterior coat of paint; the owner's brand was often sketched on the freshly covered surface.

GLOVES

All men wore gloves in cold weather; this of course to keep the hands warm. In warm weather most men wore gloves when roping—this to prevent bums or blisters from the raw rope—and wore them also when riding bucking horses, this to avoid manual injury. But some men, regardless of temperature or the nature of their work, wore gloves all the waking hours. The hands of such men frequently were as white and soft as those of a young girl.

The gloves were sometimes of horse-hide or smooth, surfaced leather, but usually were of buckskin. Whatever the material, they customarily were yellow, gray, or a greenish creamy white or brown.

They had to be of good quality, lest they stiffen after a wetting. An unduly stiff glove well might misdirect a lariat throw, or even cause a man to miss his hold upon the saddle horn when he attempted to mount a plunging horse.

Practically all gloves had flaring gantlets of generous size, and were commonly embroidered with silken thread or with thin wire of silver or brass, and being edged with a deep leathern or buckskin fringe along the little-finger side. The designs for such embroidery followed principally geometrical forms.

When the thermometer was very low, either gloves or mittens of knitted wool or of fur made their appearance.

BOOTS

The cowboy's boots were of fine leather and fitted tightly, with light, narrow soles, extremely small and high heels. Surely a more irrational foot-covering never was invented; yet these tight, peaked cowboy boots had a great significance and may indeed be called the insignia of a calling. There was no prouder soul on earth than the cowboy. He was proud of being a horseman and had contempt for all human beings who walked. On foot in his tight-toed boots he was lost; but he wished it to be understood that he never was on foot.

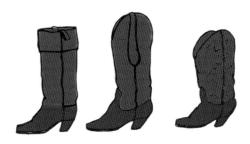

These boots had vamps of the best quality of pliable, thin leather, and legs of either like material or finest kid. The vamps fitted tightly around the instep, and thus gave to the boot its principal hold, and the legs were quite loose about the wearer's entrousered calf. The boots' legs, coming well up toward the wearer's knees, usually ended in a horizontal line, but sometimes were so cut as to rise an inch or so higher at the front than at the back. The legs often showed much fancy stitching. A *concha* or an inlay of a bit of colored leather might appear at the front of each bootleg at its top.

The boots' heels, two inches in height, were vertical at the front, and were in length and breadth much smaller at the bottom than at the top.

The tall heel, highly arching the wearer's instep, insured—as did the absence of all projections, outstanding nails, and square corners from the sole—against the wearer's foot slipping through the stirrup or being entangled in it. The tall heel also so molded the shod foot that it automatically took in the stirrup so as to bring the leg above it into proper fitting with the saddle's numerous curves. The heel's height and peg-like shape together gave an effective anchorage to the wearer when he worked afoot, instead of from his horse's back. The sole usually was quite thin. This gave the wearer a semi-prehensile "feel of the stirrup."

The conventions of Range society permitted to the buckaroo at any formal function no footgear other than this riding boot. It was as obligatory for him at a dance as it was useful to him when ahorse.

SPURS

Spurs were a necessary implement when on horseback, and a social requirement when afoot. It's sometimes said that the cowboy, when in public, would as readily omit his trousers as his spurs. Well, perhaps.

His spurs were of a build far heavier than those common in the Eastern sections of the country. Their rowels were very blunt, as they were intended as much for a means of clinging to a bucking horse as for an instrument of discipline. This help in clinging was augmented in many spurs by adding to the frame of the spur, a blunt-nosed, up-curved piece, the "buck hook," which rose behind the rider's heel, and which was used to engage or "lock" in the cinch or in the side of a plunging horse. Ordinarily, the rowels were half an inch in length, the spokes being slightly larger in diameter than a present-day twenty-five-cent piece; but spurs imported from Mexico, had two-and-a-half-inch wheels with rowels of corresponding length, and often were used in the Southwest as a matter of course.

Each spur, was held in place by two chains passing under the wearer's instep, and also by a "spur-leather" which was a broad shield of leather laid over the instep. This spur-leather also tended to protect the ankle from chafing, and was often decorated with a *concha* and stamped with intricate designs. The shank of most spurs turned downward, allowing the

buck hook, if there were one, to catch without interference by the rowels, and also permitting the wheel, when the rider was afoot, to roll noisily along the ground. This noise could be increased by disconnecting from the spur one of the two chains at one of its ends and allowing it to drag, and also by the addition of "danglers." Danglers were inch-long, pear-shaped pendants loosely hanging from the end of the wheel's axle.

A cowboy moving across a board floor suggested the transit of a knight in armor.

CHAPS

Not more specialized than the spurs but more conspicuous were the *chaparejos*, universally called "chaps." They were skeleton overalls worn as armor to protect the rider's legs from injury when he was thrown or when his horse carried him through sagebrush, cactus, or chaparral; but also they were proof against both rain and cold wind.

Take a pair of long ordinary trousers, cut away the seat, sever the seam between the legs, and fasten the whole thing to a broad belt, tied or buckled at the wearer's back, and you have a pattern for a pair of chaps. Reproduce your pattern with scraped (de-haired) heavy leather, or else in a shaggy skin of a bear, wolf, dog, goat, or sheep, and you have the real article.

You must, of course, make your pattern very loosely fitting.

Should you make your chaps of scraped leather, cut it so that a long fringe will hang from the leg's seam. You might want to cover this seam with a wide strip of buckskin.

The long hair or wool on a pair of shaggy chaps represented not so much artistic preference as it did a judgment that by this means protection would be increased. Naked leather cannot be relied upon to withstand the stab of either the yucca's pointed leaves or the spines of the tall cacti.

When not in use, the chaps were rolled in a bundle and carried tied behind the cantle of the cowboy's saddle, or packed away in the tools wagon. Chaps are heavy and they are bulky and they are not much fun to have to deal with. Back at the ranch, they are most often hung from a nail in the bunkhouse; and "hung from a nail" is only a euphemism for "thrown on the floor." They are called "cow-*BOYS*" after all, and they generally "hung their clothes on the floor—so they didn't fall down and get lost."

SADDLES, ETC.

The riding saddle used on the range was known as *cow saddle*, *range saddle,* or most commonly, as the *stock saddle*. In the East it was called the *Mexican saddle* (though it might better be called Moorish rather than Mexican, because the basic design was brought to Spain from Africa over a thousand years ago), *western saddle*, or simply the *cowboy saddle*. Unless that particular form of saddle had existed, no man could have ridden the western horse in the western country under the conditions that obtained. You might well argue that the course of Western history was determined by the stock saddle.

(The cowboy called the flat English saddle a "human saddle," "kidney pad," or "postage stamp." And he regarded this design as a token of effeteness, and not a fit accoutrement for a working horse.)

THE COWBOY'S SADDLE

The western saddle, Cowboy saddle, or stock saddle is a distinct type and is comprised of the following parts:

Tree: a frame of wood covered with rawhide.
Horn: formerly of wood, now of steel, covered with rawhide.
Fork: the front part of the tree and supports horn.
Gullet: curved portion of under side of the fork.
Cantle: raised back to the saddle seat.
Side Jockeys: leather side extensions of seat.
Back Jockeys: top skirts the uppermost broad leathers joining behind cantle.
Skirts or Suderderos: (old Spanish) broad under leathers which go next to the horse.
Stirrup Leathers: broad leathers hung from the bar of the tree and from which stirrups hang.
Strings: underlying purpose to hold saddle leathers together but ends are tied and left hanging, which adds to appearance as well as usefulness in tying on things carried.
Fenders or Rosideros: broad leather sweat protectors swinging from stirrup leathers.
Rigging: middle leathers attached to tree connecting with and supporting cinch by latigos through rigging ring.
Cinch or Cincha (Sp.): a girth of horsehair, leather, cotton, or mohair strapped under horse's belly to cinch or hold the saddle on.
Rubber Cinch: an elastic cinch used in relay races to save time in changing saddles.
Cinch or Cincha Rings: on each end of the cincha.
Latigos: leather straps hanging from either side from the rigging ring, other ends run through cinch rings used to tighten up.

Stirrup: foot support usually of wood bound with iron or brass or raw-hide, sometimes all iron or brass.

Hobbled Stirrups: stirrups tied to each other by a leather thong running under the horse's belly. With stirrups hobbled, it is almost the same as if the rider were tied in the saddle and there is no play to the stirrups. Hobbled stirrups are not allowed in bucking contests.

Tapideros or Taps: leather stirrup covers which serve as protection against cold and rain, especially through wet brush or grass, from eighteen to twenty inches in length. They are mostly for effect, though some claim the stirrups ride better. In summer they are discarded.

Seat: the easiest thing to find on a saddle but the hardest to keep.

The fundamentals of all stock saddles are pretty much alike, although they vary in detail. The height and angles of the horn and cantle, and whether the seat is short or long, wide or narrow, whether it is of approximately uniform width or more or less triangular, whether it is level or sloped upward toward either the horn or the cantle or toward both, whether the horn is vertical or inclined forward, and whether its top is horizontal or is higher at its front edge than at its rear, are all matters purely of the rider's choice. But whatever the specifics, the cantle had to be high enough to prevent the lariat-thrower from slipping backward when his cow horse after the throw squatted on its haunches and braced itself. Also, followers of the Texan custom of fastening the lariat's home end to the horn before the lariat is thrown require at least a fairly high horn, as the cowboy, besides having space for himself, needs additional room for *snubbing*, because, the instant the lariat catches, it has to be wound a few turns around the horn; i.e., to be *snubbed*.

The several slight variations in shape had special names; and a saddle was designated, according to the form of its tree, as California, Brazos, White River, Nelson, Oregon, Cheyenne, etc.

The American ranchmen's saddles were built by professional manufacturers and not, as was common in Mexico, by the cowboys themselves.

STOCK SADDLE CONSTRUCTION

Extremely stout construction is required to withstand successfully the terrific strains from roping.

Upon the front end of a strongly built hardwood frame or "tree"—comprised of longitudinal "fork" and transverse "cantle"—is bolted a metal horn; and the whole, covered with rawhide, is fastened down onto a broad, curved, leather plate that rested on the horse's back. This plate is called the "skirt." Synonyms for skirt and skirts are respectively *basto* and *bastos* (from Spanish word *basto*, a pad or a packsaddle), though some men restricted these latter terms to the leather lining of the skirt, a lining known also as the *sudadero*.

On each side of the horse there lay, on top of the skirt, a leather piece that is shorter and narrower than the skirt, fitted closely around the base of the horn and cantle, its outer edges parallel with, but well inside of, the borders of the bottom and rear edges of the skirt. This leather piece is usually in two sections, the portion forward of the stirrup-leather being termed the *front jockey*, while that part aft of the stirrup-leather is called the *rear jockey*. The composite structure fitted onto the horse's back lengthwise.

Sometimes, but not often, the skirt and the rear jockey extends backward no farther than to the cantle, and then there is sewn an *anquera*, a broad plate of leather which covers the otherwise exposed portion of the horse's hips, and protects the clothing of the rider from his animal's sweat.

Usually the skirt stretches from the horse's withers to his rump, and nearly halfway down both his flanks. This has so much bearing surface that the saddle tends to remain in position even without the aid of a cinch. A large skirt was necessary when riding buckers or when roping; but for ordinary pottering about the ranch, all but a few cowpokes used a saddle the skirt of which was much smaller.

Whether the saddle has a roll is a matter of the rider's individual choice. Some men employ this attachment, others do not. A roll is a long welt that sticks out, for a third of an inch or more, from the front face of the cantle, just under its top rim. This cornice-like addition tends to keep the rider from sliding backward out of the saddle during roping and from moving skyward when his pony is bucking.

The saddle is attached to the horse either by one cinch passing under the animal at a point approximately even with the stirrups or by two cinches, respectively designated as the front and the hind or rear cinch—passing one just behind the animal's front legs, and one some twelve inches farther to the rear. Some punchers call the cinches "girths," and the rearward of them the "flank girth." Whether a saddle should be single or double rigged is a matter of its owner's preference. The single as compared with the double is more easily put on and taken off, is a bit more flexible, but it is more apt to shift position during roping and bucking and on steep trails.

Riders differ greatly in the direction and force of the thrusts that they impose on their saddles. The controlling factor is each man's method of sitting the saddle. Some riders always keep themselves not only in balance upon the horse, but also in balance with it. These riders make no pulls or pushes that subject the saddle to twisting or dislodging strain. Horsemen of this type can go for miles without retightening cinches; rarely gall their horses' backs, can always ride their steeds long distances without an undue tiring of their mounts, and except in roping or bucking or when on steep-sided hills, don't need to care whether their cinches are loose or taut. Such men are called "light riders." They each might weigh two hundred pounds and yet "ride light." And it doesn't matter whether their saddles are single or double cinched. Still other riders are by the nature of their horsemanship, forced to employ a double rig. They will on occasion get out of balance, and will rectify themselves by impulsive twists and yanks, or they will sway from side to side, seemingly indifferent to the line of the horse's motions. All this will tend to shift the saddle from its normal position. Such riders "ride heavy," must frequently tighten their latigos, and cause many a saddle sore upon their ponies' backs. These men might cling to the bucker and throw the rope as successfully as might their lighter-riding brothers but they "beefsteak" far more horses' backs and tire far more ponies.

Finally, in certain regions, the prevailing type of local horse has a chest so short and sloping to give sufficient anchorage for any but a single cinch; while in other regions, the shortness of the corresponding horses' "barrel" gives little room for the double rig.

Users of double rig are careful to observe the rule requiring that the front cinch be tightened before the rear one is pulled on. This rule is usually strictly enforced by the animals themselves. Many a tenderfoot, unmindful of this order of procedure, has heard his fellows' cheerfully guffaw, "Hey there, you've dropped something!" as he is dumped to the ground.

Sometimes with a double rig—in order to avoid a sore, or to more firmly grip a sloping chest—the cinches were crossed below the horse, making a letter *X*.

Usually the inner surface of the bastos is smooth. If so, either a shaped pad called a *corona* or else, more commonly, a folded blanket or some other padding is put between it and the horse's back. Under the corona, or blanket, for ventilating purposes a gunny-sack is placed. In some saddles the bastos' are lined with woolly sheepskin, and in such cases the padding is omitted.

The *cincha* or, as usually termed, the cinch is a broad band made of coarsely woven horsehair or canvas or cordage, and terminates at either end in a metal ring. On each side of the saddle-tree is attached, for each cinch, a second metal ring called the rigging ring, tree ring, or saddle-ring. From that is hung a long leather strap called a *latigo*. This strap, after being passed successively and usually twice through both the cinch ring and the corresponding tree ring, is fastened below the latter by much the same method as a "four-in-hand" necktie is knotted. The latigo on the saddle's off side is permanently left fastened, and in saddling and unsaddling, operations are restricted to the strap on the near side.

(A variation of this method of fastening the latigo is often used on the near side during the breaking of a horse. In that case a wide, metal buckle offers a speedier means of attachment and release. Haste being desirable when the steed is plunging.)

The rough cinch adheres well to the horse's body and offers a good hold to the rowels and hooks of the spurs. While the cinch is, strictly speaking, merely the broad band, the term customarily is applied to the combination of both this band and its own two latigos.

The two leaves of the stirrup-leathers are looped through the tree and hang vertically form each side of the saddle. The end of the longer leaf is passed through the stirrup's top, and then made fast to the bottom of the shorter leaf. A buckskin thong, threading a series of holes in the two leaves, provide a means of fastening and an ability to adjust length. A thong is used instead of a buckle because whenever possible the use metal is avoided.

The cowboy not only wished his outfit to be able to be immediately repaired, but he had faith in the durability of leather and little faith in that of metal. He might put up with the use of buckles on saddles used for breaking horses in the corrals near the ranch house, but he wished no buckles under him when he was riding far afield. (It was this reliance upon simplicity as the best guarantor of sureness that made him prefer his pistol to be of single, rather than of the slightly more complex double action.)

Each stirrup-leather hangs from the saddle tree, and meeting almost behind the horn, rest in shallow grooves cut in the wood of the tree. In some saddles, the seat's leather covering, starting forward from the cantle, goes only to this groove's rear edge. In other saddles, this covering extends over the entire seat and completely hides the upper portion of the stirrup-leathers. The names given to these two forms of seat covering are, respectively, the *three-quarter seat* and the *full seat*. A flat leather plate—known as the *leg-jockey*—covers the spot where the stirrup-leather appears from the saddle's side and serves to protect the rider's leg from chafing. Sewn to the back of each stirrup-leather is a vertical, wide leather shield, the *rosadero*; sometimes, though often incorrectly, called the *sudadero*. It protects the rider from the horse's sweat and offers a stout defense to the rider's leg.

At the bottom of each stirrup-leather is a stirrup made of a wide piece of tough wood bent into shape, bolted together at the top, so sturdily as to defy crushing by a falling horse. Into the stirrup went the rider's foot clear to his boot's heel, his toe pointing inward, either horizontally or downward. The sides and front of the stirrup were ordinarily enclosed by a wedge-shaped leather cover, open toward the rear. The technical name for this cover was *hapadero*, though colloquially this almost always is shortened into *tap*. Commonly each side of each of the "taps" is in the form of a triangle with the apex pointing downward. Some men used taps, which followed the historic Spanish model and were shaped somewhat like horizontally laid coal-scuttles. The taps prevent the rider's feet from passing completely through the stirrups, being snagged by brush, or being bitten by a savage horse. Open stirrups, i.e., tapless ones, are rarely seen on the Range.

From each side of every saddle hang four sets of thongs, two thongs in each set. One of these sets is at the saddle's front, one near its rear, while the other two are spaced so that the rider's leg just passes between them. The two sets of rear thongs embrace whatever might be laid across the saddle behind the cantle, almost invariably the slicker, a long raincoat of oilskin; though in the Southwest, the thongs instead are used to tie off a Mexican *serape*. The front and side thongs are used to lash anything of movement. If the saddle were being used in desert country, then a pair of felt-covered, metallic canteens or two water bottles of leather or of coated canvas might hang from the horn.

Because the shape and large bearing surface of the stock saddle has so good a hold on the horse's back, except on fractious animals or in mountainous country, riders often let the cinches sag loosely. This permitted the horse to breathe more easily.

The cowboy saddle is not suitable for racing. It is too heavy, thirty pounds at the very least and usually forty pounds or more. But the usual and useful gaits of the Range have nothing to do with racing. They are the running walk, the jiggling trot, the lope, with now and then a short dash after errant livestock.

Nevertheless the western saddle was ideal for the service in which it was used.

It made wholesale roping possible. It made it possible to ride the American bucker. It made possible long and compulsory rides on animals so indifferently broken as to have been unserviceable under a less secure seat. And it served him on "the night herd," because it permitted the tired cowboy to sleep while still ahorse. Repeatedly men on herding duty were, because of storm or other circumstance, kept at their task for forty-eight consecutive hours. In the wild nights of winter, the most courageous puncher did not dare to permit his pony chance of escape, so there were catnaps in the saddle, rather than more restful sleeps beside a picket pin.

This saddle offers its occupant the opportunity to sit in perfect balance, and on such a seat as is best suited to the character of the riding involved. The mounted cowboy, at first sight and at high speed, looks grotesque. His elbows are extended to either side, his hands close together and under his chin, his shoulders bobbing up and down, and his legs hung loosely and straight downward. His relaxed body never rising from the saddle, seems to sway in semidrunkenness. But look again and you will understand that what you are really seeing is a near miracle of synchronicity of man and horse.

SADDLE DECORATION

The leather of the entire saddle, including the taps and stirrup-leathers, is often covered with handsomely impressed designs of leaves and flowers. A saddle, if so decorated, would cost, in the decades of the 1870s and '80s, some fifty dollars. In the Southwest, sometimes not only was silver laid into the groundwork of the impressed designs, but both the horn and cantle were also ornamented with precious metal. Then the cost assuredly mounted. Ten months' wages often went into decoration. At least one ranch owner had a horn and cantle each of solid gold.

Often the cowboy would decorate his own saddle with brass nails or rattlesnake skin, plastered flat. The saddle's coloring was usually light brown; but sometimes, and especially in the less expensive saddles, it was cherry-red.

THE ETHOS OF THE SADDLE

Each saddle best fits its special owner, for it gradually acquires the tiny bumps and hollows that best fit his particular anatomy, inducing both comfort and security of seat. These little moldings, which so well suit the owner, will often fight the contour of a stranger's legs. Thus, each man swears by his own saddle.

A cowboy so valued his saddle, particularly after it had been broken in, that he almost never parted with it. He might go so far in a poker game as to lose his money, gun, chaps, horse, and even shirt, and then, with saddle on his back, he would strike out afoot for the ranch, still cheerful and with "his tail up."

Moreover, it is considered a bit disgraceful to sell one's saddle. It is akin to selling off the family farm or disposing of the ancestral plate and family jewels. The phrase "He's sold his saddle" became general usage, and was employed in a figurative way to denote anybody who has become financially or morally insolvent.

PACKSADDLES

The gear needed is, for each horse or mule, a packsaddle, woolen blankets, pack cinch, thirty-five or forty feet of manila rope, another rope of the same size, twenty feet long, a pair of *alforjas*, a pair of hobbles, and a bell to put on the animal when it is turned out for the night.

A packsaddle consists of two crosses of hardwood, fastened to two flat, round-end pieces of wood, and to this is attached breeching, breast straps, and usually two cinches, and other necessary strap work.

A good packsaddle is strong and well made, of good materials. The leather is a peculiar kind that will not tighten when tied into knots, for the cinch adjustments are usually tied instead of fastened with buckles. When selecting a packsaddle, be sure that the breeching and breast straps are long enough for any horse on which the saddle may be used.

Be certain also that the saddle fits the horse reasonably well, or it will cause trouble. Most of the packhorses used on the trail are more or less hollow backed, and the saddle base should not be too long or it will rest on the ends only. On the other hand, if too short it will not be so stable and will also hurt the horse. The double cinch saddle, such as shown in the illustration, is by far the best.

Alforias are sacks that hang on the sides of the saddle. All small artifacts of the outfit are typically placed in them. They are made of very heavy duck, leather bound, and have straps or loops of rope with which to suspend them from the saddle forks. The proper size is about twenty-four inches wide, eighteen inches high, and when opened out, nine inches deep.

When packing an outfit, the horse should be tied and the blanket should be folded and placed on the horse's back. It should not be less than four folds thick and should extend a little ahead and a little behind the saddle base. It must also come down far enough on the sides to form a pad for the *alforjas* or panniers to keep them from rubbing and chafing the animal.

The saddle is then placed on the folded blanket. At this point, if you want to be kind to the poor horse, grasp the blanket between the two pieces of the saddle base and pull it up a little, so that it is loose over the horse's back. This will allow the saddle to settle down under the weight of the pack and not bind, which it is sure to do if the blanket is not loosened a little. Then both cinches should be tightened and the breeching and breast straps properly adjusted.

The panniers are then filled with the small articles of the camp equipment and hung on the forks of the saddle. If the packer is at all conscientious, he will see that each sack is of the same weight and that there are no hard or sharp objects so placed that they will injure the animal. Articles which are too big to go into the sacks are then placed on top, where they will rest firmly and not hurt the horse. Any really big objects like blankets and tent are folded and spread over the top of saddle and panniers.

At this stage commences what is generally considered the trick of packing: tying the pack to the horse. There are many forms of pack hitch in use. Any of them of them may be learned quite easily by an observing person, but nevertheless tying a pack properly can scarcely be done at the first attempt. The most popular of pack ties is what is known as the diamond hitch, and all things considered, is probably the best on the list.

To throw the diamond hitch, proceed as follows: having tied one end of the long rope to the ring of the pack cinch, go to the near side (left) of the horse and throw the cinch over the pack and horse, then reach under the horse and pick up the cinch. The hooked end of the cinch is now toward you. Draw back on the rope until you have all of the slack and pull the rope down on the near side to the hook of the cinch; double it here and give it a twist, then hook the loop to the cinch. Now double the free portion of the rope and shove it through under the part marked by the arrow, from the back. Now give this loop a twist to bring the free portion of the rope down farther toward the near side. Next grasp this rope at the place marked by the arrow, and draw up a part of the free rope.

All of this time you have been keeping the rope that crosses the pack fairly tight. You now go to the off side and pull loop A down over and under the pack, then come back and put loop under the pack on the near side. This will leave the hitch and it is ready for tightening. Start first by pulling the rope successively. The end of the rope is then tied to the ring in the pack cinch at the off side, and the diamond hitch is completed. The ropes should all be quite tight, and if they grow loose after a while, they should be tightened again.

There is another very simple way of tying a diamond hitch, which though not quite like the one described in detail, is the same in principle. As in the first method, the rope and cinch are thrown across the pack to the off side and the cinch is picked up from beneath the horse, then the rope is drawn up and hooked to the cinch, but the little twist is not put in the rope as in the first method. The free portion of the rope is then thrown across the pack to the off side so that it is parallel with and behind the first rope. Then double this rope on the top of the pack and push it under the first rope from the rear. Now bring this loop back over and push it through again forming the small loop. Now take the free end of the rope down under the pack on the near side, back and up at the rear, through the loop again. The free end of the rope then goes down under the pack from the rear on the off side and fastens to the cinch ring. The rope is tightened the same as in the other method. This hitch is as good as the other and is more easily remembered, although not as easily tied as the one first described.

Either of these pack ties may be managed easily by one man, but they are tied more rapidly by two men, one standing on the off side and the other on the near side, so that neither need walk around the horse. Then there is the additional advantage in that the rope may be drawn up tight and there is no danger that it will slip, as one or the other of the men can be holding the rope all the time the pack is being tied.

In addition to the pack ties described, there is another hitch that should be learned, as it is useful for securing packages to the packsaddle when *alforjas* are not used (also for holding packs to the sides of the saddle while tying the diamond hitch). Keep in mind that there are several methods of fixing a sling rope.

For this purpose the shorter length of rope is used. It is doubled in the middle and looped around the front forks of the packsaddle, then one-half of the rope is taken to the near side and the other is dropped on the off side. Taking either half of the rope, you allow sufficient slack to hold the pack at the proper height, then bring the rope around the rear forks, then down to the center of the slack portion, where it is tied. The pack is then fixed in this loop and the other side is arranged the same way. After both packs are properly slung, the ends of the rope are brought up on top and tied together.

There are many forms of pack hitches other than those described, although the diamond hitch is most often.

A packhorse should never be overloaded, and the animal cannot carry as great a load as many people expect. Two hundred pounds is the limit for any pack, and one hundred fifty pounds is a more reasonable load. For long journeys the pack, per horse or mule, should not weigh this much. A hundred or one hundred twenty-five pounds is all that should be allotted to any animal.

A pack train may consist of any number of pack animals, and if there are enough riders in the party, one man rides between each two packhorses. One rider goes ahead, leading a horse behind him. That horse is followed by another rider, then another packhorse, etc. If there are not enough men in the party for this, two pack animals are placed between two riders. The men may lead the horses if they are inclined to wander from the route, but ordinarily this is not necessary, as the animals will keep in line. But if you lead a packhorse, do not grow tired of holding the rope and tie it to the horn of the saddle. This is a dangerous practice and may result in serious injury, for the packhorse may become frightened and bolt or may swing around, wrapping the rope around the rider.

Pack animals are always more or less troublesome, and the man who uses them should have a bountiful supply of patience. At night the animals are hobbled, which means that their front feet are fastened together with hobbles, so that they cannot travel fast or far. Too much dependence should not be placed on these retarders, for western horses soon learn to travel quite rapidly when thus impeded, and will sometimes set out for home while the master sleeps. A good practice is to picket one or two horses in the best spots of pasture to be found, and hobble the remaining animals. They are not so likely to leave if this is done, and if they do, the picketed horses must remain behind, which insures at least a mount with which to follow the runaways. Also put a bell on each horse, as this will aid in locating the animals in the morning.

On the trail, western mules and horses rarely get any food except what they can find at night or while they are not in use, and on the plains or in the mountains where vegetation is scanty, they sometimes do not get as much as they require. Under such circumstances they should not be loaded too heavily or traveled too far in a day, and it may even be necessary, on a long journey, to take an occasional day of rest to allow them to recuperate.

QUIRT

The cowboy often hung a *quirt* (from Mexican *cuarta*, a whip; and this, in turn, from Spanish *cuerda,* a cord) from his saddle horn. The quirt is a flexible, plaited leather whip, which not counting its lashes, is about twelve inches in length. Its upper end was often weighted with lead, and gave it some heft should the rider need to manage a rearing or otherwise fractious horse. To its lower end were attached two, three, or four long thongs. A loop extending from the upper end, or head, provided a means of attachment to the rider's wrist or the saddle horn.

In some parts of the country, this whip consisted of a short wooden or iron stock carrying a lash that might be as much as a yard in length.

PICKETING

Sometimes the puncher carried on his saddle a hemp-fibered stake-rope or picket-rope, or a line of woven horsehair for securing of his horse in the field. This horsehair line was useful for picketing, and laid about one's bed, was supposed to keep rattlesnakes away. Tradition had it that certainly no snake, and probably no centipede, scorpion, or tarantula, would cross its scratchy surface.

The wooden stake, which was driven into the ground and to which one end of the picket-rope was attached, was called by many Texans a *putto*, a word derived from the French *poteau,* meaning a post.

The lariat was seldom used for picketing, a good length of working rope is simply too valuable a cowpoke's tool to chance the wear and damage picket-duty might occasion it.

The cowboy world divided into two camps on the subject of picketing. One stoutly maintained that a horse's neck was the only place proper for fastening the rope, the other fiercely holding out for a front leg. Many an hour in many a place has been given over supporting or attacking the alleged merits of each system.

Although any cowboy would gladly take up this picketing debate, he ordinarily did not picket his horse at all, but instead *hobbled* it. Some men used the United States Cavalry's form of hobble: a leather cuff buckled around each of the fore legs above the pastern joint, the two cuffs being connected by a short, swiveled chain. But the majority of cowmen produced the same result by employing a wide band of cowskin or buckskin, or even more commonly, by cutting up a gunny grain sack, and knotting it to fashion the cuffs of the hobble, a twist of rope in place of the chain. With the cowskin or buckskin, a buttonhole and wooden button, or cross-stick, sometimes were substituted for the final knot.

The purpose of the picket-rope and of the hobble is to hold the fettered animal in camp. Hobbles do not always achieve this result. Many horses become proficient in a ludicrous but effective gait, whereby the hind legs walked while the front legs made short jumps forward. An adept pony would thus hop several miles in a night. Mares were the worst offenders in this hoppity-hop method of flight. To forestall this sneaky flight, some ponies were hobbled by connecting a front and a rear leg instead of the two front legs. This fore-and-aft hobbling is called *side-lining*, unless the legs tied are on opposite sides of the horse, then it is called *cross-hobbling*.

Picketing and hobbling are used only in camp. At the ranch, a horse is either corralled or turned loose to be rounded up when needed.

BRIDLE

The bridle, *headstall,* or *bridle head* is comprised of a *crown piece, brow-band, throat latch*, and on either side, a *cheek-piece*, and has no special characteristic except that frequently the *brow-band* is omitted, and often hooks, instead of buckles, are used for attaching the bit. These hooks, one on each side, are shaped like a letter *J*. The shorter stem is sewn to the bottom of the cheek-piece, while the longer stem rises vertically above the horse's mouth.

Another common form of bridle was highly specialized. It consists of a single strap, which terminates at each end in a buckle or a hook, and is fastened to the bit. The strap is passed over the horse's head and is held in place by the simple expedient of longitudinally slitting the strap enough to permit the horse's ears, or at least his left ear, to poke through the opening. In order that it's length be adjustable, the strap is usually in two pieces, which are connected by a buckle.

The reins, one on each side of the horse, are either tied together at the saddle end, or more often left untied. Most hands prefer this latter form, because with untied reins, a rider, when thrown, is spared the danger of being entangled.

A cowboy's horse is rarely made fast to anything after his rider has dismounted. Usually the reins are simply thrown directly forward over the horse's head and allowed to hang downward from the bit to the ground. He is then at liberty to wander about and graze, and will make the most of this opportunity unless the reins have fallen across a tree limb or the bar of a hitching rack. In this case the horse almost never questions appearances; and convinced that he is firmly fastened, and afraid make a pull upon his uncomfortable bit, is likely to stand patiently for hours at a time.

When the rider returns, he is careful not throw the reins over the animal's head until he is ready to mount. For the cowpony, reins thrown over its head is the signal to move. Instead the horse is led away from the rack. The rider, standing in front of the near shoulder of the animal and facing toward its tail, seizes the near stirrup with his right hand, twists it halfway around, and holds it in that position. The left hand throws the reins over the horse's head and at the same time catches the horn. At the same moment, his left foot goes into the stirrup, the right hand grabs the horn or swings wide, and the rider is snapped into the saddle.

If the horse is prone to "back" or lunge to the rear, the ride might grab the bridle's left cheek piece with his left hand, taking hold of the horn with his right, and vaulting into the saddle. The animal's quick start is actually helpful in mounting because the sudden jerk tends to throw the rider upward and into the saddle.

When a ranchman began the process of breaking a horse, he stood on the left when placing the saddle on the animal's back, and swiftly mounted only from that side.

Ever afterward, it was on this side that the thus semibroken cattle pony expected to be approached. As a result, if the prudent ranchman needed to make a saddle adjustment on the animal's right side, he would begin negotiations from the opposite flank.

REINS

Usually before mounting, the right rein was held in shorter grip than was the left. This tended not only to prevent bites but also to swing the starting horse under the ascending rider.

In mounting the reins were kept fairly taut. A horse was more apt to buck at the moment of mounting than at any other time, and he could not buck with any effectiveness unless he was allowed to put his head between his front legs—to "stick his bill in the ground." The top of his horse's head was a pleasing sight to the man halfway into saddle.

All this has to do with mounting an already "gentled" animal, or an animal that, although never previously ridden, tacitly promises reasonably decent behavior. Mean horses were immobilized by reatas around the front and rear legs, and sometimes were blinded by a cloth tied over their eyes before being saddled, bridled, and mounted.

BITS

The bit regularly employed by the cowboy was often a thing of beauty, and always an instrument of latent torture. Artisans sometimes fashioned the cheek-pieces and the bar or chain connecting them below into intricate designs and garnished them with silver inlay. Derived directly from Mexico, the bit was often of the Spanish type, either in its design—or modified as its owner saw fit—and depending on these modifications was classed generally as a *ring bit*, *spade bit*, or *half-breed bit*.

If the bar in the horse's mouth is humped up in the middle like a narrow croquet wicket for two or two and a half inches, and within this hump, or port, there is a roller—that is a vertical wheel—and no other attachment except possibly a curb chain, the bit is called a *half-breed*.

If instead of the hump, there is a spade-shaped piece—something like a broad screwdriver—three to four inches in length and bent backward at its top, it is called a *spade bit*. This was the bit most commonly used. The severity of this bit was ordinarily augmented by inserting in the spade, at the bottom or at both top and bottom, a roller and by adding two wires closely strung with short metal tubes, extended from the sides of the spade to the inner sides of the cheek-pieces. The wires and spade punished the cheeks and the roof of the mouth. In rare instances the top of the spade was sharply notched.

Occasionally a bit employed a metal ring, fastened at the top of the port or spade and passed through the horse's mouth, enclosing its lower jaw. This ring—more common in the Southwest than in the Northwest—gradually disappeared from both regions, but remained in general use in Mexico. The presence of this ring gave to the bit, despite any other attachment it might have, the generic name of **ring bit.**

The reins were fastened, usually, not to the bit itself but to chains six inches or so in length, descending from it.

The function of the bit was to suggest physical suffering rather than to cause it. During an animal's good behavior, his reins sagged in his rider's hand, since every broken horse was **bridlewise**, and turned to right or left at the slightest pressure of the appropriate rein upon his neck.

He was thus tractable because he was always mindful of the latent possibilities of the contents of his mouth.

Stopping a well-trained pony produced almost no strain upon the reins. The stop was brought about not by the rider's pulling with his left hand, but by the raising of his right hand to the lariat-throwing position.

All **bridlewise** horses also respond to guiding signals given by the rider's legs or hands. A push on, say, the right side, if made near the animal's hind leg, would turn him to the right, while a gentle touch on the shoulder or neck would turn him to the left.

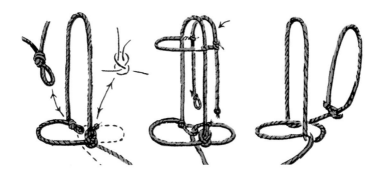

HACKAMORE

The antithesis of the severe bit was the **hackamore**.

This was sometimes an ordinary halter which had reins instead of a leading rope, and which offered to the rider no more control over his horse than mere pressure on the animal's neck might effect. More commonly it was a bridle that had, in lieu of a bit, a rawhide, or metal ring around the horse's head immediately above the mouth. The pulling of the reins operated to shut off the horse's wind.

The hackamore, even when rigged to the limit of its efficiency, did not possess the bit's cruel possibilities, but was commonly used on the first ridings of a horse in the process of being broken. Some riders continued its use on their broken animals, ruling their horses more through exercise of human personality than through mechanical means.

GHOST CORD

The *ghost cord* is a thin string tied around the tongue and gums, and then passed below the lower jaw and up to the rider's hand. It is cruel instrument.

ROPE WORK

FROM THE SPANISH

Lariat is an Americanization of *la reata*, Spanish for "the rope."
Lasso is an Americanization of *lazo,* Spanish for a noose or
snare. This term is not used by the cowboy to designate a
"catch" or "throw" rope. The tenderfoot may be identified by
his misuse of the term.
Lazo reata is the Spanish word for a "snare rope."
Reata is the Spanish word for "rope," but to North American
cowboys, it means a "rawhide rope."

The word *lariat* is of Spanish derivation. *La reata* was a
long rawhide rope used by the Mexican *vaqueros,* and was
made of twisted strands of rawhide cut from green cow or
buffalo hides. Because of the difficulty of twisting the strands
and getting them to lie close, each to the other, the rope-
makers switched to using braided rope. Four, six, or eight
strands were used in plaiting the ropes. And twisted rope made

the best sort of *reata* because of its superior strength and smoother running surface.

The dexterity of the Mexican ropers impressed the North American cowboys and their *reata* was soon adopted. But the rawhide rope was not designed for fast tying to a saddle horn as are the grass (vegetable fiber) ropes used by modern-day cowhands; tied hard and fast, it does not stand up well against the weight of a roped steer. The twisted **Manila** was much cheaper to make and can be easily tied to a saddle horn without much chance of breaking it.

VARIOUS ROPES

Ropes of various types are shown on the next page, along with some idea of how they are constructed.

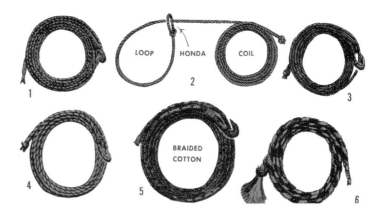

LOOP HONDA COIL

1 2 COIL 3

4 BRAIDED COTTON 5 6

Figure 1 illustrates the rawhide *reata*. It is usually about sixty feet in length. It can be thrown further, with less energy, and retains the most perfect loop of any other type of rope. But because it cannot stand the shock when tied off, hard and fast, to half a ton of plunging cow, this type of rope is, more or less, no longer used.

A well-made rawhide *reata* lasts longer than any other type of rope, but it requires a lot more attention in order to retain its vitality. It must be frequently examined for wear, and is kept waterproof and pliable by greasing it with tallow.

Figure 2 illustrates the component parts of a **catch rope**: **loop, honda,** and **coil**.

Figure 3 illustrates a maguey rope, Mexican made, from the fiber of a maguey plant. It's an excellent line for calf roping and for making horse catches, and for trick-roping.

Figure 4 illustrates a silk **Manila**, which is a hard-twist rope, and is the most popular and widely used catch rope. It is the most dependable all-round type for roping purposes.

Linen ropes, made like the hard-twist **Manila,** are also very good for roping. Many consider it the strongest line made for roping.

Figure 5 illustrates a braided cotton rope, sometimes known as a spot cord. It is most often used in trick and fancy roping and other exhibition work. It's not practical for use in regular range work.

Figure 6 illustrates a *mecate*, or hair rope, made from mane and tail hair taken from horses. Hair ropes are sometimes used for cattle roping, but because of their weight, they are generally used as tie ropes on halters and hackamores.

CARRYING THE ROPE

When not in use, the rope is gathered into a coil some eighteen inches in diameter and hung from a spot below the base of the saddle horn, on whichever side its owner prefers. The coiled rope is held in position by passing a looped thong through the hole in the center of the coil, the two ends of which are permanently attached to the saddle, or else a strap, one end of which is likewise attached, and then dropping the loop over the horn.

HONDA

A **honda** is the small eye at the loop-end, through which the rope passes to form the loop. The **honda** most used is the tied one. The best ones hang straight from the end of the rope.

There are several metal versions of **hondas**, even in use today, but the knotted **honda** remains the one most favored by real cowboys. First, a metal **honda** must be spliced, a tricky and time-consuming task. Then, the metal Honda is too free running, and because of its weight, tends to close the loop too quickly. Also, it is dangerous to the eye of any animal it happens to hit.

TYING THE HONDA

This knot is easily tied and very like a slip-knot, except that the end passes over the main line and through the center as illustrated below.

The trick to seating and tightening the **honda** is also easily managed—once you get the knack of it:

Place a stick through the knot. Stand on the stick, with your feet on both sides of the knot, and squat. Wrap the rope once around your hips and hold the rope tightly in your hands. Rise, straightening your legs and the **honda** will tighten and seat itself. Trim the end of the rope, so that it will not impede the running of the rope through the **honda**.

NEW ROPES

New ropes ought to be stretched just after the Honda and knots have been tied. This can be accomplished by stretching the new line between two corral posts. Be certain to take out all the twists and kinks as you proceed. A pole is often used to lever the slack out of the rope. Place the pole somewhere near the center of the rope to be straightened, run one end of the pole back and forth between the posts, pulling the high end of the pole down across the rope, and after sufficient back and forth, tying it off so that the rope is kept taught. Leave overnight, and when the rope is taken off the fence in the morning, it will be in a fit condition to work.

THE DALLY

Dally is a word derived from the Spanish *dar la vuelta*, and Americanized into *dally-welta*, or dally. It means to take a turn, or to wrap around an object, in this case a saddle horn. Dallying is easier on stock that are being roped, and on the saddle horse, too, because the slight give in the rope mitigates just a little the jarring stop felt by both animals when the loop closes and the rope goes taut. Dallying has the further advantage of permitting a quick release, should an accident or mishap occur; and is, on the whole, safer for both man and beast.

Old Mexico was *dally-welta* country; this is made clear by taking a look at the saddle horn used there, which makes an almost perfect snubbing post to dally a rope on. The larger the saddle horn, the more surface is in contact with the rope and the easier it is to hold a wrap. The small metal saddle horn is not a great surface to dally because the very short turns that need to be taken and because of the slickness of its surface.

THE LENGTH

The length of a catch rope varied from place to place, depending on the imperatives of custom and its use. In a state like Texas, where the custom is to tie the rope to the saddle horn, the rope runs about thirty-five feet in length. In places where the catch rope is most often dallied, it is longer. An all a round average for the North American Cowboy puts it at about thirty-five to forty feet in length. The Mexican *vaquero's* leather **reata** was much longer, sometimes as long as sixty feet.

THROWS AND CATCHES

Rope throws and catches are made in a variety of ways, according to the nature of the work at hand.

THE OVERHEAD

The overhead swing is probably the most often used catch, and is generally used in roping stock from a horse. The roper brings the loop around in a horizontal circle above his head and throws it over the head of the animal he aims to catch, as seen on page 126. Mostly, this throw is made from the saddle, and only rarely by a puncher afoot.

THE HOOLIHAN

On the other hand, the hoolihan catch is a throw most often made from the ground, as in catching horses in a corral, but may also be used in roping calves from a horse, as seen below.

The position of the loop may be horizontal or vertical, or any angle in between.

At the start of the action, the loop is held at the roper's side. He makes one revolution before the throw, as in the next illustration.

PITCH AND SLIP CATCH

The pitch catch is the simplest of throws and is almost always thrown from the ground. In this catch the loop is not rotated, but is simply held behind the roper, and then is tossed over the head of the cow or horse.

The slip catch is the preferred throw for catching a moving horse by the forefoot, but may be used just a effectively in roping an animal's head. **Forefooting** an animal only requires a little judgment in placing the loop before the moving cow or horse. In order that the loop has time to open, it should be placed three or four feet in front of the moving animal. In roping the head, it is only necessary to raise the loop high enough for the animal to run into it.

The chief difference between a pitch cast and a slip cast is that the rope travels vertically when thrown in a slip cast, and horizontally in a pitch cast.

FOREFOOTING

In **forefooting** from horseback, the roper begins the throw with the loop carried horizontally, above his head. Once he is alongside the cow, he tosses the loop slightly forward and over the shoulder on opposite side of the animal, turning his hand so that the top of the loop drops and swings in front of, and catches the escaping steer high up on its forelegs. Nearly simultaneously, the rider veers sharply away, flipping the animal onto its side when the rope reaches its limit.

In **forefooting** from the ground, the roper rolls the loop in front of the running animal, jerking the loop closed on the horse or cow's front legs. If the horse or cow to be roped is stationary, the roper rolls out a vertical loop on one side of the animal, at the same time, the roper moves sharply toward the opposite side, causing the animal to shy away and step into the loop.

HEELING

Catching a horse or cow (most often a calf) by the hind legs is known as **heeling**. The roper rotates the loop vertically and when the moment is right, calmly slips it under the animal, closing the loop with a quick wrist action once both hind legs have entered the loop. This catch is most often used in nabbing a calf in order to drag it to the branding irons.

READING TRAIL

"Tracking: Preserving your scalp by tying it to your brain."
—Jim Bridger, Mountain Man

The act of following a track, be it a man or a four-footed animal, is founded upon the same principals as those used by native peoples throughout the West, and later by hunters, trappers, army scouts, and lawmen. The cowboys called it simply "trailing" or "riding sign." Many cowboys became proficient in this art, and any good outfit boasted at least one or two punchers who were very good at it. But for the ordinary cowboy, working the open range, the task was mostly a matter of riding sign after wandering stock. Old markings are called "old sign" and make for a "cold trail" while we call recent ones "fresh sign," and they make for a "hot" or "fresh trail." Clearly visible signs make a "plain," and indistinct sign a "blind trail." If a quarry's trail has been trodden on by an animal or person, it is said to have been "fouled."

FUNDAMENTALS OF TRACKING

Since no two species of animal—man included—leave similar trails, so also no two individuals of that species leave trails that are wholly alike.

Trailing involves keen observation, and a careful reasoning from the facts of that observation, in light of what is known of the psychology of the human or animal quarry.

The powers of observation employed were, in the order of their importance: sight, hearing, scent, and touch.

When the trail is obvious to even the tenderfoot, then the task is easy, but when the facts, as it were, on the ground are few and far between, then trailing rises to the level of an art.

The tracker's work might have one of two objectives, either the overtaking of a living—again be it a man or an animal—fugitive, or else the reaching of a definite place. Each of these objectives call for differing methods. For success in the case of a pursuit, the quarry's course must be pretty much strictly followed. Although sometimes, when the chase has continued long enough to satisfy the pursuer's mind as to the quarry's intended destination, shortcuts across country might safely be hazarded.

When the tracker or scout's aim has only to do only with the reaching of a geographical objective, his work is then concerned with two propositions: first, how surely to get to that place, and second, how best to avoid all intermediate obstructions. In this he is not interested, as is the explorer, in actually mapping the details of the intervening country, though the scout may give some attention to them in so far as they might promise to be factors in the job at hand, or in some future one.

For success in the art of pursuit, the trailer first concentrates on the face of the country through which his quest is to lie, in order that, becoming familiar with the normal appearance of all the details, his attention is instantly arrested by any deviation from that normality. Once acquainted with the usual appearance of things, the trailer confines his observation to watching for the unusual. In trailing, these are the clues that write the story of the quarry's journey and prophesy his destination.

Of course the simplest pursuit involves having and keeping the fleeing animal or man in sight until overtaken, but this does not rise to the dignity of trailing.

SIGHT AND SOUND

An otherwise invisible fugitive might disclose his position by unwittingly permitting sunlight to reflect from some bright object worn upon himself or upon his horse. On brilliant days this flashing in the clear air of the West is visible for miles. For this latter reason, pursuers and pursued avoid wearing or carrying anything that might throw off a reflection. For the tracker, bright nickel and polished silver are hazards, whether it be on rifle, pistol, spur, or bit, and white shirts and handkerchiefs are shunned. The flashing from a reflecting object is particularly noticeable when that object is in motion. Because of this, the instant the trailer thinks himself observed, he stiffens himself to immobility and remains still for as long as he believes himself under observation.

The route of the man or animal pursued may be seen by impressions left underfoot or at the trail's side, by foreign objects dropped in the way, or by the fugitive's routing of birds and animals and sending them flying or scurrying into the pursuer's sight. It may be audibly reported by the fugitive's footfalls, the rolling of stones or the breaking of sticks, and if the fugitive is a man, by the discharging of his weapons. Finally, it may be reported to the nose by an identifying odor, and to the sense of touch by the temperature of dropped objects. These memoranda of travel can be read, and when cannily considered, they disclose the identity of the quarry, his route and, except in cases of the audible messages, the time elapsed since he has made any given "sign."

The impressions left underfoot might show as more or less clear imprints of the foot, as scratches upon a rocky a frozen surface, or a sun-baked soil, as breaks in sticks or vegetation, or as displacements of natural objects from their usual positions.

Because the fugitive's footprints are the best evidence of his identity, the first function of the tracker is so to acquaint himself with the impressions of his quarry's feet as to be able thereafter to distinguish them from all other tracks. To accomplish this, he might, until he came upon a set of complete imprints, have to rely on a composite construction made up of a heel's impress here, a toe's print there. A half-dozen fragmentary impressions might be all an expert trailer needs to see before he has formed an accurate, detailed conception of a foot's shape, size, and characteristics.

When the prints are once clearly pictured in the mind of a skilled tracker, he can follow them across nearly all surfaces, and through myriads of other and conflicting tracks by recognizing the telltale peculiarities that are from time to time disclosed, on this print a worn heel, in that impression a twisted toe.

If the trailer does not know the physical peculiarities of his quarry's feet or their horse's shoeings, he quickly learns them from the imprints. The size and shape of each foot, also lameness, deviations from normal pointing of the toe, undue weight thrown upon any special portion of a foot, length of stride, projecting seams, indented breaks, each is the signature of his quarry. The form, size, and character of sewn seams, a repairing patch, an unmended tear or hole leaves, for the human moccasin or boot, a record as instructive as would the broken shoe or a malformed hoof of a fleeing horse.

Limping not only drives a lame leg's foot more deeply into the ground than a sound leg sends its foot, but also is apt to cause both a twisting on the sole and a variation from the normal length of stride. Drunkenness and physical exhaustion each are recorded by prints that show successive staggerings. Just as undue indenting, here of the heel, there of the toe, signal inequality in length of stride.

Length of stride is liable to be unequal. Usually the right foot takes the longer step, the direction being maintained by twisting on the longer-stepping foot as the other was in the air. This twisting imprints a distinctive swirl upon the track. Some men bring down their feet with an even pressure while walking. Others stress upon either heel or toe.

A running man rarely touches to the ground any part of his foot except back of its ball.

A man afoot, if heavily laden, markedly indents his heels.

A ridden horse tends to cling to a fixed course. A riderless horse wanders.

A horse, when walking or trotting, makes two parallel lines of hoof-marks, one with his two right feet, the other with his two left feet.

In each of these lines are seen widely and regularly spaced sets of imprints; each set consists of the closely adjacent impressions of the front and hind feet that belong on whichever side of the horse is the one to which the line is related. Each set shows, for the normal horse, the hind foot's impression slightly in advance of that of the front foot; while a lame animal is apt on his infirm side to reverse this order. The intervals between the sets of normal prints are for a horse, when walking, approximately five feet, and when trotting, approximately eight feet.

Walking horses, when riderless, make such indentations as show the heels and toes of all four hoofs, equally impressed. But the walking horse, when ridden, acts as did any trotting horse ridden or not, and tends to accent the impressions of its toes. Trotting hoofs tend to scarf up the ground immediately ahead of them.

In the lope, and also in the gallop, all four hoofs tend to track in a single line.

A loping horse, if leading with his right front foot, makes hoof prints in the following order: (1) right front, (2) left hind, (3) left front, (4) right hind, (5) right front again.

The length of the intervals between the several impressions depends on the individual peculiarities of each animal; and also, in the case of each animal, varies with the levelness or hilliness of the course, and the character of the footing. For the average, normal horse on level ground with good surface, the intervals are approximately twenty-four inches.

In the gallop the order of imprints changes, and for a horse leading with his right front foot, was (1) right front, (2) left hind, (3) right hind, (4) left front, (5) right front again.

The intervals are much longer than in the case of the lope.

In both the lope and the gallop, if the animal were to lead with his left foot, the serial orders above given would be correspondingly transposable.

Sometimes the surface trodden upon is rock or ice, and incapable because of hardness of taking a complete impression. Nevertheless it will, from an iron horseshoe, a stone caught in the hoof, or a nail in a boot's sole, receive scratches that, from their freshness, stand clearly forth to an observant eye. In granitic rock, recently scored mica shines like a galaxy of little stars, and ice-cuts will for a time display scintillating crystals.

Freshly broken sticks leave evidence as to both the fact of passage and the identity of the fugitive pilgrim.

Unless through occasional inadvertence or when in the recklessness of terror, wild animals never step on avoidable sticks.

Logs laying across the trail are apt to receive scratches from the overstepping foot of a man or of a large-hoofed animal; and also are likely to leave broken bark and branches or stubs.

Grass or weed, trodden upon by man or a weighty animal, is usually so bruised as for some time to remain at least partly down. While it remains depressed, it tells the direction which the traveler has taken. A man usually kicks knee-high or taller grass away from him, and thus the top of depressed plants point to the direction in which the man has gone. But a large-hoofed animal, by reason of the semicircular sweep of its front feet, drag the tops of high grass backward. In this case these tops point toward the direction from which the animal has come.

Sticks or stones that have been kicked out of their normal positions on the trail will appear from the unweathered, sharply defined contours of their former beds.

Foreign objects seen on the trail tell their own story. They might include a bit of leather, a stone carried in a hoof and later dropped, a leaf or branch or flower that had adhered awhile to a boot, a spur, or a saddle strap, and then fallen off, a piece of charcoal that had for some time clung to clothing, sand collected on the foot at a stream's crossing and thereafter drying had been gradually discarded, anything that nature herself did not put upon the trail.

Scat dropped by animals and the clots of blood shed by a wounded quarry often offer valuable information, but the amateur trailer should guard against mistaking the crimson burn imposed by frost on various kinds of leaves for blood stains. Blood-clots tend to dry quickly and change their showy redness to an inconspicuous black.

Birds and loose animals, disturbed by the fugitive and fleeing from him, not only reveal the fact of his motion, but also advertise his course. Crows are the most useful of these wild allies. They will fly promptly at a man's approach.

Every mounted trailer keeps close watch upon the horse beneath him. The Range pony is alert to all movements, sounds, and odors; and, by his suddenly cocked ears, his quickly erected head, and his sniffing, might direct the rider's notice to the quarry, or to some factor indicating its whereabouts.

Sometimes the pony's nose has to be held in order to stifle the whinny that is apt to call out to the quarry's mount. To avoid giving himself away, the tracker often needs to avoid approaching directly from the quarry's windward, lest his scent drift on the breeze to a sensitive nose.

Hearing is also important, but only when within a fairly close distance from the fugitive; though the audible radius might greatly be increased by the scout's putting his ear to the ground. The sound of a moving horse, particularly when the animal is moving rapidly over hard ground, can in this way be distinguished from quite far away, and distinguished so clearly as to disclose the identity of the gait of the beast, whether a trot, a lope, or a gallop.

At close range the kind of noise coming from breaking sticks tells much about who is fracturing them. Horses, cattle, and men, with their ruthless motion, tend to produce sharply sounding cracks, but all wild animals, however large, have a more stealthy step, and produce a slower, more crunching, and less insistent breaking noise. Wet sticks and dry ones sound quite dissimilar.

Canvas or corduroy, when rubbed upon itself, on rocks or on tree branches, emits a telltale sound. For this reason Indian scouts refused to include these materials in their clothing.

Sounds from firearms advertise the approximate position of the quarry, and often tell the identity of its creator. The quantity of the noise betrays the distance it has traveled. The wind's direction and force are often factors as well, since the wind might be either an aid or a hindrance to the transit of the sound.

With black powder, no two rifles, even though of the same make and caliber, produce sounds identical in character. Some occult difference in their steel differentiates their noises. And between weapons of unlike calibers, the difference in sound is very evident. If the trailer is familiar with the report of his quarry's weapon, a single shot will often indicate the fugitive's identity.

THE SCENT OF THE CHASE

The trailer's sense of smell often reveals the presence of the campfire of his quarry, and also sometimes permits him to identify the ownership of objects dropped on the trail. Tanned buckskin might, through long usage or rough treatment, change its appearance, but it never can rid itself of its characteristic odor. A tobacco user might have all his belongings so permeated with the weed's smell that his handkerchief or piece of cloth lying along the way might speak more definitely to the nose of the tracker than to his eye.

The tracker's sense of touch is also useful in judging the time elapsed since the pursued has passed by, whether it be a question of the relative warmth of an abandoned campfire, the hardness of a print in the earth, or the softness of horse droppings on the trail.

THE AGE OF THE TRAIL

There are some simple effects of nature's processes that give definite information as to age.

Grass growing on dry soil, and trodden-down but not severely bruised, will quickly rise to erect position when later wet by rain or dew. Grass growing in moist soil, and likewise stepped upon and fairly uninjured, will also promptly straighten and become vertical. But, in an arid country with a burning sun, vegetation, flattened after the heat of the day had commenced, will lie for hours prostrate, much of it to wait for the coming of the next night's dew.

Dew, and still more markedly rain, by their action on the ground's surface, aids an observer in gauging the age of tracks. Falling moisture wipes out the sharpness of all prior markings, and gives the surface of the bare soil a smooth finish. Any cut on that finish obviously has been made after the finish had been created.

The edges of charcoal rounded under the slightest stress from wind or water, gives a good idea as to the date of an extinguished fire. Still smoldering wood or steaming ground betrays a more recently abandoned camp.

Often a footprint of the quarry merges with an imprint made by some other person or animal. If the trailer knows, as he often does, the age of the foreign track, he can be certain which print is atop the other.

THE PSYCHOLOGY OF THE QUARRY

Pursued persons or animals frequently resort to certain subterfuges for escape. These include:

Entering running streams or other bodies of water, traveling for a distance in the water, and then returning to the land.

For men, the ascent of trees, and the travel for a time through the treetops before returning to the ground and resuming ordinary motion.

For men, stepping successively on top of the bulges of the bases of the trunks of growing trees, and by finding handholds on these same trees, swinging from tree to tree.

But, in most cases:

A human quarry will not follow a straight course for any considerable distance, but will attempt some subterfuge.

If he is merely seeking safety and not hurrying to a definite goal, he will leave a stream on the same side on which he has entered. Whether he will turn downstream or up will depend on the position of his pursuers and on the qualities of the stream. If the pursuers were to one side of the quarry, the latter almost surely will proceed in the direction away from the side of his pursuers, but if the pursuers are to his rear, he will almost certainly start in whichever direction a hurried glance at the stream's bottom suggests will give the speedier footing.

A man taking to the treetops will turn back on the course that he had been following on the ground, and unless hurrying to some definite place, will ultimately leave the forest on the same side in which he had entered it.

A man swinging from tree to tree will circle his way from his earlier course, and on reaching the ground, will have reversed his initial direction.

This trick of doubling back to deceive seems to be part of our nature. Look at children playing games of pursuit. Watch any boy at play and you will see this is the case.

But if the cowboy keeps his eyes and ears open, is alert and observant, and uses his common sense, he is very likely to get his quarry, even if it is only a lost steer.

THE COWBOY BY PHILIP ASHTON ROLLINS

THE REVOLVER

When you recall that the gun actually carried—when one was carried—was the forty-five or forty-four caliber, eight-inch barreled, single-action Colt revolver, weighing two and a quarter pounds—and that its ammunition weighed something in addition; when you recall also that the average cowboy was not an incipient murderer, but was only an average man and correspondingly lazy, then you realize why he was unwilling to encumber himself with more than one gun, and why he often even failed to "pack" (carry) that unless conditions made it necessary.

These necessary conditions were first, an expectation of attack by a personal enemy; second, work near the Mexican border or in Indian country; third, work on a range where he might meet human trespassers, or encounter animals dangerous to stock or stock hopelessly injured or diseased.

The cowboy carried the revolver in a commonplace holster openly hanging from a loose belt. He very rarely engaged in the tricks that in popular fiction are so often attributed to him: no attaching his pistol to a cord and hiding in his shirt, no firing from the hip, through the holster's tip without pausing to withdraw the pistol, no filing the revolver's mechanism to produce a "hair-trigger," no rapid fanning or brushing the hammer with his palm.

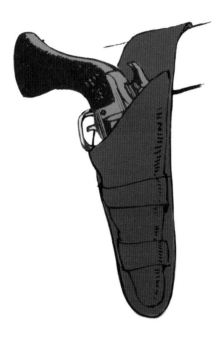

These variations from the normal were, in fact, not uncommonly employed by officers of the law, by bandits—all men who hunted other men—and were, in fact, sometimes in the presence of tenderfoots ostentatiously "showed off" by braggarts.

But in fact, were very rarely made use of by the cowboy. He kept his solitary weapon at his side (his right or left side, depending on whether he was right- or left-handed) butt to the rear, and in the clearly visible holster. When he wanted to shoot, he simply pulled out the pistol and shot it. The cowboy, however, did take pains to use a holster, which, having no covering-flap, offered to the pistol speedy and easy egress. He took pains also to see that none of his clothing should intervene between his hand and his pistol's butt.

He did not touch the bolstered weapon, or even, in the language of the novels, "feel for it" until he was prepared to fire, otherwise an absentminded fingering of the weapon might lead to an accident, or give an armed enemy good reason for firing the first shot. Moreover, the pistol was an instrument for shooting and not for making mere threats.

Incidentally, no old-timer, having "gotten the drop" on a man and wishing to disarm him, would for an instant have thought of asking the prisoner to do what some modern western writers have required of him, to "Hand over your gun, and do it butt toward me." The old-timer knew that butt first meant a finger dangerously near the trigger-guard, that a finger through that guard and a quick snap of the wrist would "spin" or "flip" the gun, that in the fraction of a second its muzzle would point forward. So the old-timer ordered his prisoner merely to drop his weapon and to back away from the spot where it lay on the ground.

The cowboy shot, if he thought it necessary, and then without hesitation. When he shot, he shot with intent to kill; but his bullets rarely struck another man. The cowboy may have disliked to have another person "ride him," or "run over" him, but the average puncher did not kill out of pique, or in defense of mere personal pride.

However prosaic it may seem, one half of the West did not spend its time in either "getting the drop" or "pulling down" on the other half, or even in "looking for somebody." Nor did the cowboy "notch" his pistol's butt.

As compared with men, the cowboy was no better or worse a marksman than innate aptitude and the extent of target practice made him.

Nevertheless he materially advantaged himself by disdaining the short-barreled, top-heavy, erratic pistol of the townsman, and by habitually using the long-barreled, perfectly balanced Colt. It was because of the faultless "hang" or balance of this weapon that the cowboy's shooting reputation was made. The weapon's balance helped both accuracy and speed, for it relieved the shooter from the necessity of eyeballing the sights. Aiming a Colt was akin to pointing a forefinger.

The average cowboy was a relatively better shot with the pistol than with the rifle. He used the pistol with more frequency, and had greater interest in its potentialities.

The cowboy's gun had plain wood in its stock. The novelist has supplanted it with carved ivory or mother-of-pearl. The metal of the cowboy's gun was colored black or dark blue. The novelist has nickel-plated it.

For the purpose of self-defense the gun was no more potent than often was the unflinching eye of a man with an established reputation for steady nerves and for ability to "draw quick and shoot straight."

THE RIFLE

The rifle was rarely carried except when there existed one of the serious conditions already mentioned, or where there was big game to be shot. The rifle, was carried, not by the cowboy himself but conveyed by his horse, which bore it in a quiver-shaped, openmouthed scabbard, into which the rifle slipped up to its stock. This scabbard sometimes hung from the saddle horn, but more commonly was slung, butt forward, in an approximately horizontal position along the near side of the animal, and passed between the two leaves of the stirrup-leather.

A good enough reason for spurning it because, being heavy, it interfered with ready saddling and unsaddling, and being bulky, materially detracted from the rider's comfort.

Winchester rifle

THE WINCHESTER

After the early 1870s, the rifle, regardless of its make, was usually called a "Winchester," though this particular name, because of its similarity to the name of a well-known brand of condiment, was occasionally paraphrased into "Worcestershire." Failing these titles, the weapon was styled merely a "rifle." Except in the case of the rifles specially designed for bison-shooting and called "buffalo guns," the Winchester was never was called "gun." The word "gun," save for the single exception noted, was saved for the pistol.

"Scatter-guns," otherwise shotguns, were occasionally produced by tenderfoots; but they, unless with sawed-off "barrels" loaded with nails or buckshot, and in the hands stagecoach guards, served for the westerner only as objects of derision.

KNIVES

The last weapon to mention is the knife. After the earlier Indian fighting had ceased, long knives were rarely carried by cowpunchers unless they were hunting big game, or were

Mexican in blood or spirit. A stout pocket jack-knife, or clasp-knife, was most useful.

The long knife in the hands of a competent user was, within a range of thirty feet, the deadliest weapon of the West, for pulled and thrown, it usually would reach its goal before the opponent's pistol could be drawn and shot, and this though the thrower and shooter simultaneously started to act. In a hand-to-hand fight, the knife was driven by an underhand thrust, edge up, into the abdomen, and was terrible in its effect. As one old-timer said: "The knife is a plumb ungentlemanly weepen, and it shore leaves a mussy-looking corpse."

COWBOY JUSTICE

LAW, WRIT AND UN-WRIT

The cowboy had a fair sense of right and wrong. But justice in the kingdom of cattle was often a scarce commodity, especially out on the range where the arm of the "law" did not reach.

HORSE AND CATTLE THIEVING

To steal a cowboy's horse was about the worst thing you could do to him, worse than stealing his money—he was usually broke anyway—and more objectionable even than kissing his girl—he didn't know many nice girls.

It sounds faintly comic to our modern ears, but horse thieving was regarded as a real outrage. And while horses willingly were lent, nobody but a thief would take one—even temporarily—unless with the owner's clear say so, or unless the taker was in real difficulty, a distress so genuine that he dared risk that the obvious truth of it would later exculpate him.

Robbing a rider of his horse easily might cause—in bad country—the cruelest kind of death; so the people out west—in self-defense—refused to allow a thief to plead that his stealing had been in any way justified, or that the crime had not put any one afoot, and with a common voice prescribed the punishment. Horse stealing earned death by hanging, or if the vigilance committee were tolerant, life banishment from "these parts." This exile was often preceded by loss of the upper half of an ear, an earmark that branded a man, and lasted to the grave.

Long hair might cover the scar, but long hair in itself was regarded with some suspicion, a vague suggestion that the fellow might be hiding something; or else as indicating a desire to be—in appearance though not in fact—"tough and wild." Consequently long hair did not meet with general approval. A man with a "load of hay on his head" might be an actual "bad man," but usually he was diagnosed as being weak-minded or a "bluffer." Long hair was of course permissible to any one who wished to grow it, but extravagantly long hair was suspicious.

The punishment for horse stealing was promptly extended to include the taking of cattle; though cattle thieves ordinarily were more leniently dealt with, and when raiding for political reasons, as in Wyoming's "Rustler War," were often pardoned and even praised by the broader public.

THE RUSTLER

No character on the range was ever more fully discussed or less fully understood than the rustler. Many people are familiar with the verb "to rustle," and know what it means when one is asked to "rustle a little wood" for the campfire, or when it is announced that the horses should be turned out to "rustle a little grass," but they would be unable to give the original derivation of the term "rustler."

Any one acquainted with the cattle country soon heard a lot about the rustler. He heard of the murder of some dweller in an outlying camp, and he was informed that the crime was attributed to "rustlers." A stagecoach might be held up, or a train robbed, and the act would be laid at the door of this same mysterious being—the rustler. He might hear that a number of men had been the victims of a lynching bee, and be advised that the men hung were rustlers. In time he might come to believe that any and all bad characters of the West were called "rustlers."

But this would be inaccurate and unjust. The real rustler was an operator in a more restricted field, and although it would be impossible to get a cattle baron to believe there was ever any such thing as a good rustler, it is at least true that there were two sides to the rustler's case.

In the later sense of the term, all rustlers were criminals. In the original sense of the word, no rustler was a criminal. He was simply a hard-working man, who was paid a little gratuity for a little extra exertion on his part. He got his name in the early "maverick days," before the strict laws governing the handling cattle. Then he was a cowboy pure and simple, and sometimes his employer gave him two, three, or five dollars for each maverick he found and branded to the home brand. At the same time, the cattle associations often paid any cowboy five dollars a head for any maverick he found for the association. It behooved the cowboys of those days to "get out and rustle" for calves, the word being a sort of a synonym for the city slang word "hustle," with no bent or evil meaning attached to it. The term passed through some years of evolution before it gained its modern significance. Under the system of "maverick gratuities" the cowboy prospered. Any cowpuncher of active habits and a disposition to save could easily lay up considerable sums of money each year. And because he was bred on the range and understood nothing but the cow business, it was the most natural thing in the world for him to buy a few cows and to start in business for himself, sometimes while still under pay of his former employer, and sometimes "on his own hook."

Soon there began to be hundreds of new brands on the range, and the wealthy cattlemen saw some of their cowboys building up herds in competition with their own. It always grieves the heart of a rich man to see a poorer man begin to make too much money. So the big men met and combined against the little ones. They agreed that no more maverick commissions should be paid, and that the cowpuncher could "rustle" no more calves for himself, but should rustle them for his employer only.

Also, it was soon agreed that no cowboy should be allowed to own a brand of his own. It was at the beginning of the West of today, the humdrum, commonplace, exact, businesslike, dog-eat-dog West which is precisely like any other part of the country.

This blow at the welfare of the cowboy had a curious effect. It was intended to stop "rustling," but instead, it increased it. It was intended to protect the herds of the big ranchers, but it came near to ruining them. It was intended to help establish an honest business system, and it resulted in establishing a dishonest one. It set the written law against the unwritten law.

The rustler was a cowpuncher, and one of the best. He understood the wild trade of the range to its last detail. Among cowpunchers there were men naturally dishonest, and these turned to illegal rustling as matter of course. They were joined by the loose men who "were not there for their health."

Thus the cult of the rustler grew. The ranks were filled by cowpunchers wholly bad and only partly bad, by old-time cowpunchers and new ones, by ex-skin hunters and drifters of the range; in short, by all sorts of men who saw in the possibilities of the cow trade a chance to make a living in a way which to them seemed either excusable, expedient, or easily capable of concealment. The qualifications for this calling were simply those of the cowpuncher. The rustler must without fail be a rider, a roper, a sure shot, and fully posted in all the intricacies of marks and brands. He must, moreover, be a man of "nerve."

As there is much inaccurate popular knowledge about the character of the rustler himself, there is still less understanding regarding his occupation and the manner in which he carried it on. Really the rustler needed to be the most expert of all cow handlers, because he had to deceive the most expert of the legitimate followers of the trade, and was forced to outwit, outride, and out-brand—sometimes even to outshoot—the cowmen who had been in the business all their lives, and he needed to know the range brands thoroughly, and to know how they could most successfully be changed without detection.

It might be supposed, for instance, that the branding iron of the rustler was simply a straight "running iron," with which he wrote his own brand over the former brand on an animal; or it might be supposed that he simply impressed his own hot stencil on the hide of the creature, blotting out the original brand. This would be very clumsy work, apt to be easily detected by the nature of the wound left upon the hide of the creature, which would often slough off and leave visible proof that there had been tampering with the brand.

The rustler was very fond of a bit of hay wire, or better yet, of telegraph wire, as a branding tool. This could be folded up and put in the pocket, so it could be easily carried without much chance of detection. Upon occasion, it could be twisted into the form of almost any of the set brands of the district, or made into shapes that would cunningly alter such original brands, and yet leave no trace of the original. After the rustler had used his bit of wire, the whole altered brand had the appearance of having been a genuine brand and all made at the same time. The fresh burn fitted in with the older and heavier burning in such way that it was impossible to tell legally that there had ever been any attempt at a change.

Another favorite way of making a good-looking brand was by branding through a wet blanket. The heavy iron could then be used, and yet the wound would not be so severe as to "give the thing away" as the saying of the range ran. Experts were divided as to the merits of these two methods of blotting brands, but the easily concealed hay wire had its advantages. It was so easy to pull a bit of crooked wire out of the pocket, heat it red hot, and by simply laying it upon a given point of the calf's hide acquire title to that calf. That alone would represent a pretty fair day's work for a poor man.

If the rustler wanted any beef, he simply shot down any animal he fancied and skinned it, carrying away the meat. As he might not care to have the incriminating hide found in his keeping, with its telltale brand to speak against him, he might burn up or destroy the hide or throw it away.

It was not considered any crime at all for the residents of the country to kill what beef they wanted for their own use, provided it was beef that belonged to the big cattle companies. But the rustlers were not content with this. They wanted to do a little more than live. So they began to regularly market this free beef. A great many of the butcher shops in the ragged little frontier towns would take all the risk of handling such beef, especially if this happened to be in one of the recognized rustler towns, where a trial involving the title to beef always went one way, and that not in favor of a nonresident or a big cattle company.

Under these conditions the rustler was able to make a living and a little more than a living, and had not much cause to complain; he "had no kick coming." But presently there appeared on the horizon a change of condition that offered him a still better chance to get on in the world, and gave his occupation a veritable "boom."

Across the cattle range of Nebraska and Wyoming came the advancing arm of a railroad. The camps of the railroad contractors, where hundreds of men were employed and had to be fed, made a most enticing market, one right at the door of the rustler.

The rustler was a boon to the railroad camps, and they were a boon to him. At once a fine traffic sprung up in free beef, and whole communities benefitted by the new line of trade. Here were the cattle. Here was the market. There was no complicated system of roundups and drives and shipping and inspecting, and best of all, a man did not need any money to go into business. All he required was a rifle and a wagon. It was no wonder that under so flattering a prospect, a great many men went in with the gangs of the resident rustlers. The result was so wholesale a stealing of the range cattle of nonresidents and of large resident outfits that the industry of cattle raising received a terrible blow. All the profits of the ranches were going into the hands of the rustlers, and the herds, instead of increasing, were standing still or decreasing.

REBRANDING BY RUSTLERS

It may be interesting to learn the exact manner in which brands were changed by these light-fingered persons, so that one brand was made into another without leaving proof behind it of the change.

One of the first brands to appear on the upper ranges after the first Southern drives was the old | O brand. Numbers of cattlemen bought cattle of that brand to stock their ranges, and of course, needed to rebrand the cattle. It was an easy thing to think of the | QI brand, and this was one of the largest outfits on the range. But let us suppose a rustler wanted to brand one of the | Q cows for his own private purposes. He simply took his little iron or wire, and put a little top to the figure 1, making it into a 7. It then appeared thus: 7O. Quite a different thing! Still more different was it written with a letter S after it, thus: 7OS. The owner would not recognize his own cow thus disguised. Neither could the owner of a | QI cow very well prove his property when he found it wearing a brand which said 7OI. The matter would be still more difficult by the time the next rustler had made it 7OL> and the original | O cow would be very difficult to recognize under the evolved brand HOB. It should be borne in mind that the brand mark as it actually shows upon the hide is not so sharp and clearly defined as it looks upon paper. There was a brand known on the range as the Wrench brand, thus : JC. By the time the rustler was done with it, it appeared thus: Q Or it might assume this form, QJJO and be called the Bridle-bit brand. The brand 21 was easily made to read 26. Without much trouble 999 could appear quite differently, as 888 The hair of the cow would cover up any little defects of penmanship. A brand which was a simple V was easily altered, as thus : A; but the skilful rustler would have been wise enough to put a straight line across it, thus : -A- covering up the junction mark of the two brands.

Of course this was all a serious injury to the legitimate trade. Those ranchmen who were suffering soon joined forces to crush out this growing evil, which otherwise must have put an end to the cattle trade. The whole sanctity of the brand was going.

Finally came the climax of affairs, which ultimately resulted in the defeat of the rustler and the general establishment on the range of those principles of justice which were agreed on as best for the interests of all. The cattle associations attained the practical control of the cattle business.

The rustlers were wrong. They were lawless men, refugees, and outlaws many of them. Yet there is a certain picturesqeness in their story, intimately bonded as it is with the story of the cattle trade and of the cowboy. It was the rustler who held the last pinnacle in the fight for the old days and the old ways of the West. Since his fight was doomed of necessity to he a losing one, let us at least endeavor to be just to him.

He was the burglar of the range; but, unlike the burglar of the cities, he very often thought that he was justified in what he did by the precedents of his country. When he came to see and to believe that he was wrong, he in many cases reformed and never again went back to the old ways. There should be no stigma allowed to rest upon the name of as honest and hard-working a class of men—men who at one time were "a little on the rustle."

VIGILANCE COMMITTEES

The vigilance committee of the cowboy era was no hotheaded lynching party out to claim a victim. Instead it was the people acting directly, instead of through their formally elected or appointed representatives. It gave due process of law commensurate with frontier conditions, and aimed to support, not to subvert, justice.

That seriousness underlaying the whole matter can be seen from the fact that the vigilance committees often accorded their prisoners actual, if informal, trials, often acquitted, and when convicting, frequently prescribed as the penalty banishment and not death. Then, too, when death was prescribed, the committees, with respect for law's long-established usages, subjected the prisoner to hanging done with orderliness and decency.

It is true that the vigilance committee sometimes killed with bullets, but it was only when the accused, resisting arrest, "put up a fight."

Tradition relates that on rare occasions men were lynched because they erroneously had been supposed to perpetrated a particular crime with which in fact they had had no connection, but tradition adds that each such victim was known to have performed at least one other act which by itself would have warranted the rope. So, while there may have occurred an error in judicial process, there had been none in moral result, even though some bad man might seem merely to have been "hung on his merits."

A vigilance committee rarely advertised what it had done, or where or how "the event" had occurred, and always sacredly guarded deathbed confessions of guilt. No nonattendant at the final scene would, if wise, question any man on the subject who had been present there. This meant on the part of the committee's members no cowardly screening of themselves from the officers of statutory law. Merely, the West considered lynching, however necessary, to be a nasty job, and did not like to talk about it.

However, despite the ban of secrecy, history by chance has recorded the last words of a few lynched men.

Boone Helm, about to be hung at Virginia City, Montana, and standing beside the gallows on which writhed the body of one of Boone's gang, made this little speech:

"Kick away, old fellow. I'll be in hell with you in a minute. Every man for his principles! Hurrah for Jeff Davis! Let her rip!"

At another time, George Shears more plaintively said: "Gentlemen, I am not used to this business, never having been hung before. Shall I jump off, or slide off?"

But the "strangulation jig" is not a pleasant subject.

COWBOY HUMOR AND PHILOSOPHY

"If you ain't made up your mind, don't use your spurs."

—Proverb

"It ain't enough for a man to learn how to ride, he must also learn how to fall."

—Mexican Proverb

"Bill stared at him. 'Does your mind hurt your head?' he asked solicitously."

—Eugene Manlove Rhodes, *The Trouble Man*

"He couldn't hit the ground with his hat in three throws."

—Anonymous

"Don't fret about biting off more than you can chew, likely your mouth's a whole lot bigger than you think."

—Unknown

"When your horse dies, get off."

—Proverb

"The word 'bronco' comes from the Spanish word for 'rough.'"

—Unknown

"You live in hell? I ride him every day!"

—Proverb

"It don't matter how big a ranch you have, or how many cattle you brand, or how many dollars you have, the size of your funeral is still going to depend on the weather."

—Unknown

"If your horse don't want to go there, then neither should you."

—Proverb

"Every tub stands on its own bottom."

—John Wesley Hardin

"It'll feel a whole lot better, soon as it quits hurtin.'"

—Unknown

"Good judgment comes from experience, and a lot of that comes from bad judgment."

—Unknown

"You can't get lard 'less you boil the pig."

—Unknown

"The worst troublemaker you're ever likely to meet, watches you shave his face in the mirror every morning."

—Unknown

"The wagon outfit consists of the 'Chuck Wagon' which carries the food bedding and tents, and from the back of which the food is prepared over an open fire. The 'Hoodlum Wagon,' which carries the water barrel, wood and branding irons, furnishes the Chuck Wagon with water and wood, the branding crew with wood, and attends all round-ups or branding pens with a supply of drinking water."

—Walter Prescott Webb, The Great Plains, 1931

"During the war his clothing was made from homespun cloth, he had no other, home-made shoes or boots, even his hat was home-made, the favorite hat material being straw. Rye straw was the best. Sometime a fellow would get hold of a Mexican hat, and then he was sailing."

—W. S. James, *Style on the Ranch*

"Every cowboy furnishes his own saddle bridle, saddle blanket, and spurs; also his bedding, known as a 'Hot Roll,' a 16 to 20 oz. canvas 'Tarp' about 18 feet long doubled and bedding in between, usually composed of several quilts known as 'suggans' and blankets—rarely a mattress, the extra quilts serving for mattress. The top 'Tarp' serves as extra covering and protects against rain."

—Frank S. Hastings, *Some Glimpses into Ranch Life*

"The cowboy's outfit of clothing, as a rule, is one of the best from hat to boots, he may not have a dollar in the world, but he will wear good, substantial clothing, even if he has to buy it on credit, and he usually has plenty of that. I once heard a minister in a little Northern town, in using the cowboy as an illustration, say 'The Cowboy with an eighteen dollar hat and a two dollar suit of clothing is as happy as a king on his throne.' In fact, extravagance is one of the cowboy's failings."

—W.S. James, *Style on the Ranch*

"Whiskey has been blamed for lots it didn't do. It's a brave-maker. All men know it. If you want to know a man, get him drunk and he'll tip his hand. If I like a man when I'm sober, I kin hardly keep from kissing him when I'm drunk. This goes both ways. If I don't like a man when I'm sober, I don't want him in the same town when I'm drunk."

—Charles M. Russell, *Whiskey*

"My idea of a good cow-boss is a man that doesn't boss any; just hires a first-class outfit of men, and then there is no bossing to do."

—Andy Adams

"Whoever said a horse was dumb, was dumb."
—Will Rogers

"Horses?"
"Yeah, horses. You know. The things you fall off of."
—*Ride, Ranger, Ride*, 1936

"I like a damned fool," he hissed; "but you suit me too well!"
—Eugene Manlove Rhodes, *The Trouble Man*

"How to ride a horse: First, you mount the horse. Second, you stay mounted."
—Proverb

"He couldn't hit the ground with his hat in three throws."
—Anonymous

"Never approach a bull from the front, a horse from the rear, or a fool from any direction."
—Proverb

"Mister, I wouldn't set that coal-oil on the stove. It ain't judicious."

—Anonymous

"A smart ass doesn't fit in the saddle."

—Unknown

"A man, a horse and a dog never tire of each other's company."

—Proverb

"Leo," said Jeff, "you're a good boy—a mighty good boy. But I don't believe you'd notice it if the sun didn't go down till after dark."

—Eugene Manlove Rhodes, *The Trouble Man*

"Don't leave your saddle out in the rain."

—Unknown

"When you lose, don't lose the lesson."

—Proverb

We had camped on a high divide west of the Judith River, about fifteen miles from the river, where there were a number of big springs, Charlie Russell was as lousy as a pet coon. Pete Vann and Bill Skelton told him to pull off all his clothes and lay them on some anthills nearby.

"Will that take care of the situation?" asked Charlie.

"Yes, the ants will eat all the lice," Bill Skelton answered.

Charlie pondered over this a second or two, then began undressing, putting his clothes on the anthills. The first thing he pulled off was his hat, then his coat and shirt, then off went his pants, lastly his boots. The ants sure had a feast and devoured all the lice. Bill Skelton and Pete Vann walked down to the roundup wagon, bringing back some cottonwood sticks and boards. They drove the stakes into the ground, tied the boards to the sticks with some rawhide strings, took a piece of charcoal from the fire and printed this sign:

Louse Creek Bench

This bench is known by that name to this day.

—Bob Kennon, *Charlie Russell*

"I prefer a safe horse to a fast one—I would like to have an excessively gentle horse—a horse with no spirit whatever—a lame one if he had such a thing."

—Mark Twain

"When I was a kid, if a guy got killed in a western movie, I always wondered who got his horse."

—George Carlin

"There's something about riding on a prancing horse that makes you feel like something, even when you ain't got a thing."

—Will Rogers

"He's yellow as mustard, but without the bite."

—Anonymous

"As we go to press, Hell is in session in Ellsworth."

—*Kansas State News*, 1873

"My mother and sisters thought my prowess with the gun was just a little tomboyish."

—Annie Oakley

"You haff last request?"
"Sure would like me a chew of tobacco."

—*Hang 'Em High*, 1968

"Brother, when I hit 'em they stay hit."

—Gabby Hayes, *Bordertown Gun Fighters*, 1943

"If lawyers are dis-barred, and clergymen are de-frocked, don't it follow that cowboys are de-ranged?"

—Unknown

"The Bible says when a man smites you on one cheek to turn the other, so I done that. Then I didn't have any further instructions, so I used my own judgment!"

—Eugene Manlove Rhodes, *Aforesaid Bates*

"Speak your mind, but ride a fast horse."

—Proverb

"Fast is fine, but accuracy is everything. Take your time. It's important to draw first and get off the first shot, but it's much more important to have your shot go where you want it to go."

—Attributed to Wyatt Earp

"The old West is not a certain place in a certain time, it's a state of mind. It's whatever you want it to be."

—Tom Mix

"If you're not making dust, you're eating it."

—Proverb

"Just because it's a well-marked trail, doesn't mean whoever made it knew where he was going."

—Proverb

"'Bout as easy as milkin' a bull."

—Anonymous

"Humorous writers tell us that it was a breach of good manners to ask a man his name, or what State he was from, or to examine the brand on his horse very particularly. It can be safely said that there was a great amount of truth mingled with the humor. Some of these fugitives from justice became good citizens, but the majority sooner or later took up former callings."

—Andy Adams

"A bad day roping beats a good day at any other work."

—Traditional Cowboy Saying

"Western fieldwork conjures up images of struggle on horseback."

—Stephen Jay Gould

"In the excitement of a stampede a man was not himself, and his horse was not the horse of yesterday. Man and horse were one, and the combination accomplished feats that would be utterly impossible under ordinary circumstances. Trained men can generally be found near the 'point' at both sides of the herd. When the man on one side saw the herd bending his way he would fall back, and if the work were well done on the other side of the herd the stampede then gradually came to an end; the strain was removed, the cowboys were the happiest men on earth and their shouts and laughter could be heard for miles over the prairie."

—Charles Goodnight, *Prose and Poetry of the Live Stock Industry*

"Always drink upstream from the herd."

—Proverb

"Beef cattle, that is, four year old long horns differ greatly from other cattle in their travel. The first day after being put out on the trail they will travel twenty-five miles without any trouble then as the pace begins to tell on them they fall back to fifteen or twenty miles a day, and there also seems to be an understanding among the cattle themselves that each must take a turn at leading the herd, those that start in the lead in the morning will be away back in the center of the herd at noon, and those that started in the center are now leading. This they keep up until all have had their turn at leading and as a rule if they are not scared by something they will stay pretty well bunched."

—Nat "Deadwood Dick" Love

"When you add it all up, the worst hardship we had on the trail was loss of sleep. Sometime we would rub tobacco juice in our eyes to keep awake."

—Teddy Blue Abbot

"Before starting out on the trail, I made it a rule to draw up an article of agreement, setting forth what each man was to do. The main clause stipulated that if one shot another he was to be tried by the outfit and hanged on the spot, if found guilty. I never had a man shot on the trail."

—Charles Goodnight, Legendary Cattleman

"And God said, let the earth bring forth the living creature after this kind, cattle and creeping things, the earth after his kind; and it was so."

—*King James Bible*

"This is the finest fence in the world. It's light as air, strong as whiskey, and cheaper than dirt!"

—John W. 'Bet-a-Million' Gates, Texas barbed wire salesman

"It took all hands, and the cook."

—Unknown

"Only a fool argues with the cook."

—Anonymous

"That there coffee'd melt a spoon!"

—Traditional Cowboy Chuck Wagon Grumble

"But Pecos Bill found a cheaper way of makin' post holes."
"'What was his new method?' asked Lanky.
'Why he jest went out and rounded up a big bunch of prairie-dogs, and turned 'em loose where he wanted the fence, and of course every critter of 'em begun diggin' a hole, for it's jest prairie-dog nature to dig holes. As soon as a prairie-dog would git down about two feet, Bill would yank him out and stick a post in the hole. Then the fool prairie-dog would go start another one, and Bill would git it. Bill said he found prairie-dog labor very satisfactory. The only trouble was that sometimes durin' off hours, the badgers that he had gradin' would make a raid on the prairie-dogs, and Bill would have to git up and drive 'em back to their own camp.'"

—Moody C. Boatright, *Pecos Bill*

"There were only two things the old-time cowpunchers were afraid of: a decent woman and being set afoot."
— E. C. "Teddy Blue" Abbott

"Cowboys weren't allowed to kiss girls in pictures, so one time I gave Dale a little peck on the forehead and we got a ton of letters to leave that mushy stuff out . . . so I had to kiss Trigger instead."
—Roy Rogers

"So we mostly size a fellow up by his abilities as a trouble man. Any kind of trouble—not necessarily the fightin' kind. If he goes the route, if he sets to the limit, if he's enlisted for the war—why, you most naturally depend on him."
—Eugene Manlove Rhodes, *The Trouble Man*

"Judge Roy Bean was said to conduct marriages for $5 and divorces for $10. When he was informed that he surely did have the authority to conduct marriages but could not grant divorces, the Judge reposted. 'I have the right to undo any wrong I have done.'"
—Traditional Western Anecdote

"Timing has a lot to do with the outcome of a rain dance."
—Proverb

"I wouldn't mind going broke so much," said Dick Mason, "but I sure hate to see the cattle die, and me not able to do the first thing to save them."
—Eugene Manlove Rhodes, *Aforesaid Bates*

"I must say that the 'cow-punchers' as a class, maligned and traduced as they have been, possess a quality of sturdy sterling manhood which would be to the credit of men in any walk of life. The honor of the average 'puncher' abides with him continually. He will not lie; he will not steal. He keeps faith with his friends; toward his enemies he bears himself like a man. He has vices—as who has not?—but I like to speak softly of them when set against his unassailable virtues. I wish that the manhood of the cow-boy might come into fashion further East."
—Frederic Remington, *Life in the Cattle Country*

"Above all things, the plainsmen had to have in instinct for direction. I never had a compass in my life, but I was never lost."
—Charles Goodnight, Legendary Cattleman

"A cowboy was not educated, but he received lessons from contact with Nature and the hardships of life which qualified him to think for himself and know how to measure men by correct standards. He was laconic in speech, using few words to express himself, but his meanings were forceful and easily understood by his comrades. He wore serviceable Stetson hats, shop-made boots, costly overshirts and usually a silk handkerchief around his neck. The real old-time cowboy of my time never went gaudily dressed as they now do in the picture-shows."

—H. H. Halsell, *The True Cowboy*

"Sometimes the demands were so urgent that a man's boots would not be taken off his feet for an entire week. The nerves of the men usually became wrought up to such a tension that no man was to be touched by another when he was asleep until after he had been spoken to. The man who suddenly aroused a sleeper was liable to be shot, as all were thoroughly armed and understood the instant use of the revolver or the rifle."

—Charles Goodnight, *Prose and Poetry of the Live Stock Industry*

"I wanted someone to kill me, so concluded to go to the Black Hills."

—Charles Siringo, *On a Tare in Wichita, Kansas*

"Yer durn tootin'!"

—Gabby Hayes

COWBOY SONGS

As for singing, the cowboy was fond of music, or rather that kind of humanly created noise that on the Range stood in for song. Musical gatherings, so called "sings," were popular.

Except for banjos, and the occasional infirm fiddles— each of these instruments often having only a few surviving strings—and except for mouth-organs, Jew's harps, and an occasional accordion, there was little besides the human voice with which to make music.

In this singing, nasal tones predominated, and songs were rendered usually with considerable seriousness, both of sound and of facial expression. Variations in high notes and long, drawn-out notes were deeply loved.

The favorite songs had numerous stanzas, and in lugubrious terms referred to home or dying mothers. Wording might vary with geography, but loneliness most often was the theme. "The Home I Ne'er Will Live to See" and "I'm a Poor Lonesome Cowboy" vied in popularity with other dirges such as "The Night My Mother Passed Away." It required some ten minutes for the classic "The Dying Cowboy," to recite his pathetic history and arrive at the point where, with every note held so long as breath endured, he "laid himself down beside the trail and died," or in another version, appealed: "Oh, bury me not on the lone prairie."

At times mournfulness was laid aside, and great pleasure was derived from ditties like "I've Found a Horseshoe." Here again sentimentality prevailed, as in "Rosalie the Prairie Flower," or so much of "Annie Laurie" and like ballads as the singers could remember.

Among the few cheerful bits of music were "Roll on, roll on, roll on little doggies, roll on, roll on. Roll your tail, and roll her high. We'll all be angels by and by," and that chant, "The little, old, gray horse came tearing out of the wilderness." In this song, the animal never arrived at his destination because whenever the singers brought him to the edge of the wilderness, a long-drawn, unctuous "and" brought the singers back to the song's initial words, automatically replacing the little, old, gray horse at his original starting-point with some other animal.

The cowboy most often retired early; for so hard was the day's work that ranch evenings were very short and bedtime followed closely on the heels of supper. There was little incentive to fight off drowsiness because there was scant light in which to stay awake. Kerosene lamps were the only illumination, and ill-kept lamps indoors and smoky lanterns outdoors were not much good. Candles, and even torches of fat pine, were substituted in simple establishments far from the railway, and the inhabitants of such primitive places ordinarily hit the sack before darkness set in.

"SONG OF THE CATTLE TRAIL"

The dust hangs thick upon the trail
And the horns and the hoofs are clashing,
While off at the side through the chaparral
The men and the strays go crashing;
But in right good cheer the cowboy sings,
For the work of the fall is ending,
And then it's ride for the old home ranch
Where a maid love's light is tending.
Then it's crack! crack! crack!
On the beef steer's back,
And it's run, you slow-foot devil;
For I'm soon to turn back where through the black
Love's lamp gleams along the level.
He's trailed them far o'er the trackless range,
Has this knight of the saddle leather;
He has risked his life in the mad stampede,
And has breasted all kinds of weather.
But now is the end of the trail in sight,
And the hours on wings are sliding;
For it's back to the home and the only girl
When the foreman OK's the option.
Then it's quirt! quirt! quirt!
And it's run or git hurt,
You hang-back, bawling critter.
For a man who's in love with a turtle dove
Ain't got no time to fritter.

"A NEVADA COWPUNCHER TO HIS BELOVED"

Lonesome? Well, I guess so!
This place is mighty blue;
The silence of the empty rooms

Jes' palpitates with—you.
The day has lost its beauty,
The sun's a-shinin' pale;
I'll round up my belongin's
An' I guess I'll hit the trail.
Out there in the sagebrush
A-harkin' to the "Coo-oo"
Of the wild dove in his matin'
I can think alone of you.
Perhaps a gaunt coyote
Will go a-lopin' by
An' linger on the mountain ridge
An' cock his wary eye.
An' when the evenin' settles,
A-waitin' for the dawn
Perhaps I'll hear the ground owl:
"She's gone—she's gone—she's gone!"

"THE COWBOY'S LAMENT"

As I walked out in the streets of Laredo,
As I walked out in Laredo one day,
I spied a poor cowboy wrapped up in white linen,
Wrapped up in white linen as cold as the clay.

"Oh, beat the drum slowly and play the fife lowly,
Play the Dead March as you carry me along;
Take me to the green valley, there lay the sod o'er me,
For I'm a young cowboy and I know I've done wrong.

"I see by your outfit that you are a cowboy,
"These words he did say as I boldly stepped by.
"Come sit down beside me and hear my sad story;
I was shot in the breast and I know I must die.

"Let sixteen gamblers come handle my coffin,
Let sixteen cowboys come sing me a song,
Take me to the graveyard and lay the sod o'er me,

For I'm a poor cowboy and I know I've done wrong.

"My friends and relations, they live in the Nation,
They know not where their boy has gone.
He first came to Texas and hired to a ranchman,
Oh, I'm a young cowboy and I know I've done wrong.

"Go write a letter to my gray-haired mother,
And carry the same to my sister so dear;
But not a word of this shall you mention
When a crowd gathers round you my story to hear.

"Then beat your drum lowly and play your fife slowly,
Beat the Dead March as you carry me along;
We all love our cowboys so young and so handsome,
We all love our cowboys although they've done wrong.

"There is another more dear than a sister,
She'll bitterly weep when she hears I am gone.
There is another who will win her affections,
For I'm a young cowboy and they say I've done wrong.

"Go gather around you a crowd of young cowboys,
And tell them the story of this my sad fate;
Tell one and the other before they go further
To stop their wild roving before 'tis too late.

"Oh, muffle your drums, then play your fifes merrily;
Play the Dead March as you go along.
And fire your guns right over my coffin;
There goes an unfortunate boy to his home.

"It was once in the saddle I used to go dashing,
It was once in the saddle I used to go gay;
First to the dram-house, then to the card-house,
Got shot in the breast, I am dying to-day.

"Get six jolly cowboys to carry my coffin;
Get six pretty maidens to bear up my pall.

Put bunches of roses all over my coffin,
Put roses to deaden the clods as they fall.

"Then swing your rope slowly and rattle your spurs lowly,
And give a wild whoop as you carry me along;
And in the grave throw me and roll the sod o'er me,
For I'm a young cowboy and I know I've done wrong.

"Go bring me a cup, a cup of cold water,
To cool my parched lips," the cowboy said;
Before I turned, the spirit had left him
And gone to its Giver,—the cowboy was dead.

We beat the drum slowly and played the fife lowly,
And bitterly wept as we bore him along;
For we all loved our comrade, so brave, young, and handsome,
We all loved our comrade although he'd done wrong."

"THE BUNK-HOUSE ORCHESTRA"

Wrangle up your mouth-harps, drag your banjo out,
Tune your old guitarra till she twangs right stout,

For the snow is on the mountains and the wind is on the plain,
But we'll cut the chimney's moanin' with a livelier refrain.

Shinin' dobe fire-place, shadows on the wall
(See old Shorty's friv'lous toes a-twitchin' at the call:)
It's the best grand high that there is within the law
When seven jolly punchers tackle "Turkey in the Straw."

Freezy was the day's ride, lengthy was the trail,
Ev'ry steer was haughty with a high-arched tail,
But we held 'em and we shoved 'em for our longin' hearts
were tried
By a yearnin' for tobaccer and our dear fireside.

Swing 'er into stop-time, don't you let 'er droop
(You're about as tuneful as a coyote with the croup!)
Ay, the cold wind bit when we drifted down the draw,
But we drifted on to comfort and to "Turkey in the Straw."

Snarlin' when the rain whipped, cussin' at the ford —
Ev'ry mile of twenty was a long discord,
But the night is brimmin' music and its glory is complete
When the eye is razzle-dazzled by the flip o' Shorty's feet!

Snappy for the dance, now, till she up and shoots!
(Don't he beat the devil's wife for jiggin' in his boots?)
Shorty got throwed high and we laughed till he was raw,
But tonight he's done forgot it prancin' "Turkey in the Straw."

Rainy dark or firelight, bacon rind or pie,
Livin' is a luxury that don't come high;
Oh, be happy and unruly while our years and luck allow,
For we all must die or marry less than forty years from now!

Lively on the last turn! Lope 'er to the death!
(Reddy's soul is willin' but he's gettin' short o' breath.)
Ay, the storm wind sings and old trouble sucks his paw
When we have an hour of firelight set to "Turkey in the Straw."

"RIDING SONG"

Let us ride together,
Blowing mane and hair,
Careless of the weather,
Miles ahead of care,
Ring of hoof and snaffle,
Swing of waist and hip,
Trotting down the twisted road
With the world let slip.
Let us laugh together,—
Merry as of old
To the creak of leather
And the morning cold.
Break into a canter;
Shout to bank and tree;
Rocking down the waking trail,
Steady hand and knee.
Take the life of cities,—
Here's the life for me.
'Twere a thousand pities
Not to gallop free.
So we'll ride together,
Comrade, you and I,
Careless of the weather,
Letting care go by.

"WHEN BOB GOT THROWED"

That time when Bob got throwed
I thought I sure would bust.
I like to died a-laffin'
To see him chewin' dust.
He crawled on that Andy bronc
And hit him with a quirt.
The next thing that he knew
He was wallowin' in the dirt.
Yes, it might a-killed him,
I heard the old ground pop;
But to see if he was injured
You bet I didn't stop.
I just rolled on the ground
And began to kick and yell;
It like to tickled me to death
To see how hard he fell.
'Twarn't more than a week ago
That I myself got throwed,
(But 'twas from a meaner horse
Than old Bob ever rode).
D'you reckon Bob looked sad and said,
"I hope that you ain't hurt!"
Naw! He just laffed and laffed and laffed
To see me chewin' dirt.
I've been prayin' ever since
For his horse to turn his pack;
And when he done it, I'd a laffed
If it had broke his back.
So I was still a-howlin'
When Bob, he got up lame;
He seen his horse had run clean off
And so for me he came.
He first chucked sand into my eyes,
With a rock he rubbed my head,
Then he twisted both my arms,—

"Now go fetch that horse," he said.
So I went and fetched him back,
But I was feelin' good all day;
For I sure enough do love to see
A feller get throwed that way.
S'lute yer pardners! Let 'er go!
Balance all an' do-ce-do!
Swing yer girls an' run away!
Right an' left an' gents sashay!
Gents to right an' swing or cheat!
On to next gal an' repeat!
Balance next an' don't be shy!
Swing yer pard an' swing 'er high!
Bunch the gals an' circle round!
Whack yer feet until they bound!
Form a basket! Break away!
Swing an' kiss an' all git gay!
Al'man left an' balance all!
Lift yer hoofs an' let 'em fall!
Swing yer op'sites! Swing agin!
Kiss the sagehens if you kin!"

"A COWBOY'S LOVE SONG"

Oh, the last steer has been branded
And the last beef has been shipped,
And I'm free to roam the prairies
That the round-up crew has stripped;
I'm free to think of Susie,—
Fairer than the stars above,—
She's the waitress at the station
And she is my turtle dove.

Biscuit-shootin' Susie,—
She's got us roped and tied;
Sober men or woozy
Look on her with pride.
Susie's strong and able,

And not a one gits rash
When she waits on the table
And superintends the hash.

Oh, I sometimes think I'm locoed
An' jes fit fer herdin' sheep,
'Cause I only think of Susie
When I'm wakin' or I'm sleep.
I'm wearin' Cupid's hobbles,
An' I'm tied to Love's stake-pin,
And when my heart was branded
The irons sunk deep in.

Chorus

I take my saddle, Sundays,—
The one with inlaid flaps,—
And don my new sombrero
And my white angora chaps;
Then I take a bronc for Susie
And she leaves her pots and pans
And we figure out our future
And talk o'er our homestead plans.

Chorus

"WHISKEY BILL"

A-down the road and gun in hand
Comes Whiskey Bill, mad Whiskey Bill;
A-lookin' for some place to land
Comes Whiskey Bill.

An' everybody'd like to be
Ten miles away behind a tree
When on his joyous, aching spree
Starts Whiskey Bill.

The times have changed since you made love,
O Whiskey Bill, O Whiskey Bill!
The happy sun grinned up above
At Whiskey Bill.

And down the middle of the street
The sheriff comes on toe and feet
A-wishin' for one fretful peek
At Whiskey Bill.

The cows go grazing o'er the lea,—
Poor Whiskey Bill! Poor Whiskey Bill!
An' aching thoughts pour in on me
Of Whiskey Bill.
The sheriff up and found his stride;
Bill's soul went shootin' down the slide,—
How are things on the Great Divide,
O Whiskey Bill?

"THE OUTLAW"

When my loop takes hold on a two-year-old,
By the feet or the neck or the horn,
He kin plunge and fight till his eyes go white,
But I'll throw him as sure as you're born.
Though the taut rope sing like a banjo string
And the latigoes creak and strain,
Yet I've got no fear of an outlaw steer
And I'll tumble him on the plain.

For a man is a man and a steer is a beast,
And the man is the boss of the herd;
And each of the bunch, from the biggest to least,
Must come down when he says the word.

When my leg swings 'cross on an outlaw hawse
And my spurs clinch into his hide,
He kin r'ar and pitch over hill and ditch,
But wherever he goes I'll ride.
Let 'im spin and flop like a crazy top,
Or flit like a wind-whipped smoke,
But he'll know the feel of my rowelled heel
Till he's happy to own he's broke.

For a man is a man and a hawse is a brute,
And the hawse may be prince of his clan,
But he'll bow to the bit and the steel-shod boot
And own that his boss is the man.

When the devil at rest underneath my vest
Gets up and begins to paw,
And my hot tongue strains at its bridle-reins,
Then I tackle the real outlaw;
When I get plumb riled and my sense goes wild,
And my temper has fractious growed,
If he'll hump his neck just a triflin' speck,
Then it's dollars to dimes I'm throwed.

For a man is a man, but he's partly a beast —
He kin brag till he makes you deaf,
But the one, lone brute, from the West to the East,
That he kaint quite break, is himse'f.

"THE BRONC THAT WOULDN'T BUST"

I've busted bronchos off and on
Since first I struck their trail,
And you bet I savvy bronchos
From nostrils down to tail;
But I struck one on Powder River,
And say, hands, he was the first
And only living broncho
That your servant couldn't burst.
He was a no-count buckskin,
Wasn't worth two-bits to keep,
Had a black stripe down his backbone,
And was woolly like a sheep.
That hoss wasn't built to tread the earth;
He took natural to the air;
And every time he went aloft
He tried to leave me there.
He went so high above the earth
Lights from Jerusalem shone.
Right thar we parted company
And he came down alone.
I hit terra firma,
The buckskin's heels struck free,
And brought a bunch of stars along
To dance in front of me.
I'm not a-riding airships
Nor an electric flying beast;
Ain't got no rich relation
A-waitin' me back East;
So I'll sell my chaps and saddle,

My spurs can lay and rust;
For there's now and then a digger
That a buster cannot bust.

"OLD PAINT"

Goodbye, Old Paint, I'm a-leavin' Cheyenne,
Goodbye, Old Paint, I'm a-leavin' Cheyenne,

My foot in the stirrup, my pony won't stand;
Goodbye, Old Paint, I'm a-leavin' Cheyenne.

I'm a-leavin' Cheyenne, I'm off for Montan';
Goodbye, Old Paint, I'm a-leavin' Cheyenne.

I'm a ridin' Old Paint, I'm a-leadin' old Fan;
Goodbye, Old Paint, I'm a-leavin' Cheyenne.

With my feet in the stirrups, my bridle in my hand;
Goodbye, Old Paint, I'm a-leavin' Cheyenne.

Old Paint's a good pony, he paces when he can;
Goodbye, little Annie, I'm off for Cheyenne.

Oh, hitch up your horses and feed 'em some hay,
And seat yourself by me so long as you stay.

My horses ain't hungry, they'll not eat your hay;
My wagon is loaded and rolling away.

My foot in my stirrup, my reins in my hand;
Good-morning, young lady, my horses won't stand.

Goodbye, Old Paint, I'm a-leavin' Cheyenne.
Goodbye, Old Paint, I'm a-leavin' Cheyenne.

"A BORDER AFFAIR"

Spanish is the lovin' tongue,
Soft as music, light as spray;
'Twas a girl I learnt it from
Livin' down Sonora way.
I don't look much like a lover,
Yet I say her love-words over
Often, when I'm all alone —
"*Mi amor, mi corazón.*"

Nights when she knew where I'd ride
She would listen for my spurs,
Throw the big door open wide,
Raise them laughin' eyes of hers,
And my heart would nigh stop beatin'
When I'd hear her tender greetin'
Whispered soft for me alone —
"*Mi amor! mi corazón!*"

Moonlight in the patio,
Old Señora noddin' near,
Me and Juana talkin' low
So the "madre" couldn't hear —
How those hours would go a-flyin',
And too soon I'd hear her sighin',
In her little sorry-tone —
"*Adiós, mi corazón.*"

But one time I had to fly
For a foolish gamblin' fight,
And we said a swift good-bye
On that black, unlucky night.
When I'd loosed her arms from clingin',
With her words the hoofs kept ringin',
As I galloped north alone —
"*Adiós, mi corazón.*"

Never seen her since that night;
I kaint cross the Line, you know.
She was Mex. and I was white;
Like as not it's better so.
Yet I've always sort of missed her
Since that last, wild night I kissed her,
Left her heart and lost my own —
"*Adiós, mi corazón.*"

"I WANT MY TIME"

I'm night guard all alone tonight,
Dead homesick, lonely, tired and blue;
And none but you can make it right;
My heart is hungry, Girl, for you.
I've longed all night to hug you, Dear;
To speak my love I'm at a loss.
But just as soon as daylight's here
I'm goin' straight to see the boss.
"How long's the round-up goin' to run?
Another week, or maybe three?
Give me my time, then, I am done.

No, I'm not sick. Three weeks? Oh gee!"
I know, though, when I've had enough.
I will not work— darned if I will.
I'm goin' to quit, and that's no bluff.
Say, gimme some tobacco, Bill.

"THE OLD COWMAN"

I Rode across a valley range
I hadn't seen for years.
The trail was all so spoilt and strange
It nearly fetched the tears.
I had to let ten fences down—
(The fussy lanes ran wrong)
And each new line would make me frown
And hum a mournin' song.

Oh, it's squeak! squeak! squeak!
Hear 'em stretchin' of the wire!
The nester brand is on the land;
I reckon I'll retire.
While progress toots her brassy horn
And makes her motor buzz,
I thank the Lord I wasn't born
No later than I wuz!

"Twas good to live when all the sod,
Without no fence nor fuss,
Belonged in partnership to God,
The Government and us.
With skyline bounds from east to west
And room to go and come,
I loved my fellowman the best
When he was scattered some.

Oh, it's squeak! squeak! squeak!
Close and closer cramps the wire!
There's hardly play to back away

And call a man a liar.
Their house has locks on every door;
Their land is in a crate.
There ain't the plains of God no more,
They're only real estate.

There's land where yet no ditchers dig
Nor cranks experiment;
It's only lovely, free and big
And isn't worth a cent.
I pray that them who come to spoil
May wait till I am dead
Before they foul that blessed soil
With fence and cabbage head.

Yet it's squeak! squeak! squeak!
Far and farther crawls the wire!
To crowd and pinch another inch
Is all their heart's desire.
The world is over-stocked with men,
And some will see the day
When each must keep his little pen,
But I'll be far away.

When my old soul hunts range and rest
Beyond the last divide,
Just plant me in some stretch of West
That's sunny, lone and wide.
Let cattle rub my tombstone down
And coyotes mourn their kin,
Let hawses paw and tramp the moun'—
But don't you fence it in!

Oh, it's squeak! squeak! squeak!
And they pen the land with wire.
They figure fence and copper cents
Where we laughed round the fire.
Job cussed his birthday, night and morn
In his old land of Uz,

But I'm just glad I wasn't born
No later than I wuz!

"A COWBOY ALONE WITH HIS CONSCIENCE"

When I ride into the mountains on my little broncho bird,
Whar my ears are never pelted with the bawlin' o' the herd,
An' a sort o' dreamy quiet hangs upon the western air,
An' thar ain't no animation to be noticed anywhere;
Then I sort o' feel oneasy, git a notion in my head
I'm the only livin' mortal—everybody else is dead —
An' I feel a queer sensation, rather skeery like, an' odd,
When thar ain't nobody near me, 'ceptin' God.

Every rabbit that I startle from its shaded restin' place,
Seems a furry shaft o' silence shootin' into noiseless space,
An' a rattlesnake a crawlin' through the rocks so old an' gray
Helps along the ghostly feelin' in a rather startlin' way.
Every breeze that dares to whisper does it with a bated breath,
Every bush stands grim an' silent in a sort o' livin' death —
Tell you what, a feller's feelin's give him many an icy prod,
When thar ain't nobody near him, 'ceptin God.

Somehow allus git to thinkin' o' the error o' my ways,
An' my memory goes wingin' back to childhood's happy days,
When a mother, now a restin' in the grave so dark an' deep,
Used to listen while I'd whisper, "Now I lay me down to sleep."
Then a sort o' guilty feelin' gits a surgin' in my breast,
An' I wonder how I'll stack up at the final judgment test,
Conscience allus welts it to me with a mighty cuttin' rod,
When thar ain't nobody near me, 'ceptin' God.

Take the very meanest sinner that the nation ever saw,
One that don't respect religion more'n he respects the law,
One that never does an action that's commendable or good,
An' immerse him fur a season out in Nature's solitude,

An' the cog-wheels o' his conscience 'll be rattled out o' gear,
More'n if he 'tended preachin' every Sunday in the year,
Fur his sins 'ill come a ridin' through his cranium rough shod,
When thar ain't nobody near him, 'ceptin' God.

"PINTO"

I am a vaquero by trade;
To handle my rope I'm not afraid.
 I lass' an *otero* by the two horns
Throw down the biggest that ever was born.
 Whoa! Whoa! Whoa! Pinto, whoa!

My name to you I will not tell;
For what's the use, you know me so well.
The girls all love me, and cry
 When I leave them to join the rodero.
Whoa! Whoa! Whoa! Pinto, whoa!

I am a vaquero, and here I reside;
 Show me the broncho I cannot ride.
They say old Pinto with one split ear
 Is the hardest jumping broncho on the rodero.
Whoa! Whoa! Whoa! Pinto, whoa!

There strayed to our camp an iron gray colt;
The boys were all fraid him so on him I bolt.
You bet I stayed with him till cheer after cheer,
He's the broncho twister that's on the rodero.
Whoa! Whoa! Whoa! Pinto, whoa!

My story is ended, old Pinto is dead;
 I'm going down Laredo and paint the town red.
 I'm going up to Laredo and set up the beer
To all the cowboys that's on the rodero.
Whoa! Whoa! Whoa! Pinto, whoa!

"A DANCE AT THE RANCH"

From every point they gaily come, the broncho's unshod feet
Pat at the green sod of the range with quick, emphatic beat;
The tresses of the buxom girls as banners stream behind —
Like silken, castigating whips cut at the sweeping wind.
The dashing cowboys, brown of face, sit in their saddle thrones
And sing the wild songs of the range in free, uncultured
tones,
Or ride beside the pretty girls, like gallant cavaliers,
And pour the usual fairy tales into their list'ning ears.
Within the "best room" of the ranch the jolly gathered throng
Buzz like a hive of human bees and lade the air with song;
The maidens tap their sweetest smiles and give their
tongues full rein
In efforts to entrap the boys in admiration's chain.
The fiddler tunes the strings with pick of thumb and scrape
of bow,
Finds one string keyed a note too high, another one too low;
Then rosins up the tight-drawn hairs, the young folks in a fret
Until their ears are greeted with the warning words, "All set!

S'lute yer pardners! Let 'er go!
Balance all an' do-ce-do!
Swing yer girls an' run away!
Right an' left an' gents sashay!
Gents to right an' swing or cheat!
On to next gal an' repeat!
Balance next an' don't be shy!
Swing yer pard an' swing 'er high!
Bunch the gals an' circle round!
Whack yer feet until they bound!
Form a basket! Break away!
Swing an' kiss an' all git gay!
Al'man left an' balance all!
Lift yer hoofs an' let 'em fall!
Swing yer op'sites! Swing agin!
Kiss the sagehens if you kin!"

An' thus the merry dance went on till morning's
struggling light
 In lengthening streaks of grey breaks down the barriers of
the night,
 And broncs are mounted in the glow of early morning skies
 By weary-limbed young revelers with drooping, sleepy eyes.
 The cowboys to the ranges speed to "work" the lowing herds,
 The girls within their chambers hide their sleep like
weary birds,
 And for a week the young folks talk of what a jolly spree
 They had that night at Jackson's ranch down on the
Owyhee.

"THE GAL I LEFT BEHIND ME"

I struck the trail in seventy-nine,
The herd strung out behind me;
As I jogged along my mind ran back
For the gal I left behind me.
That sweet little gal, that true little gal,
The gal I left behind me!

If ever I get off the trail
And the Indians they don't find me,
I'll make my way straight back again
To the gal I left behind me.
That sweet little gal, that true little gal,
The gal I left behind me!

The wind did blow, the rain did flow,
The hail did fall and blind me;
I thought of that gal, that sweet little gal,
That gal I'd left behind me!
That sweet little gal, that true little gal,
The gal I left behind me!

She wrote ahead to the place I said,
I was always glad to find it.

She says, "I am true, when you get through
Right back here you will find me."
That sweet little gal, that true little gal,
The gal I left behind me!

When we sold out I took the train,
I knew where I would find her;
When I got back we had a smack
And that was no gol-darned liar.
That sweet little gal, that true little gal,
The gal I left behind me!

"THE INSULT"

I've swum the Colorado where she runs close down to hell;
I've braced the faro layouts in Cheyenne;
I've fought for muddy water with a bunch of howlin' swine
An' swallowed hot tamales and cayenne;
I've rode a pitchin' broncho till the sky was underneath;
I've tackled every desert in the land;
I've sampled XX whiskey till I couldn't hardly see
An' dallied with the quicksands of the Grande;
I've argued with the marshals of a half a dozen burgs;
I've been dragged free and fancy by a cow;
I've had three years' campaignin' with the fightin', bitin' Ninth,
An' I never lost my temper till right now.

I've had the yeller fever and been shot plum full of holes;
I've grabbed an army mule plum by the tail;
But I've never been so snortin', really highfalutin' mad
As when you up and hands me ginger ale.

"THE SHALLOWS OF THE FORD"

Did you ever wait for daylight when the stars along the river
Floated thick and white as snowflakes in the water deep and strange,
Till a whisper through the aspens made the current break and shiver
As the frosty edge of morning seemed to melt and spread and change?
Once I waited, almost wishing that the dawn would never find me;
Saw the sun roll up the ranges like the glory of the Lord;
Was about to wake my pardner who was sleeping close behind me,
When I saw the man we wanted spur his pony to the ford.
Saw the ripples of the shallows and the muddy streaks that followed,
As the pony stumbled toward me in the narrows of the bend;
Saw the face I used to welcome, wild and watchful, lined and hollowed;
And God knows I wished to warn him, for I once had called him friend.
But an oath had come between us—I was paid by Law and Order;
He was outlaw, rustler, killer—so the border whisper ran;
Left his word in Caliente that he'd cross the Rio border —
Call me coward? But I hailed him—"Riding close to daylight, Dan!"
Just a hair and he'd have got me, but my voice, and not the warning,

Caught his hand and held him steady; then he nodded, spoke my name,

Reined his pony round and fanned it in the bright and silent morning,

Back across the sunlit Rio up the trail on which he came.

He had passed his word to cross it—I had passed my word to get him —

We broke even and we knew it; 'twas a case of give and take

For old times. I could have killed him from the brush; instead, I let him

Ride his trail—I turned—my pardner flung his arm and stretched awake;

Saw me standing in the open; pulled his gun and came beside me;

Asked a question with his shoulder as his left hand pointed toward

Muddy streaks that thinned and vanished—not a word, but hard he eyed me

As the water cleared and sparkled in the shallows of the ford.

"LASCA"

I want free life, and I want fresh air;
And I sigh for the canter after the cattle,
The crack of the whips like shots in battle,
The medley of hoofs and horns and heads
That wars and wrangles and scatters and spreads;
The green beneath and the blue above,
And dash and danger, and life and love —
And Lasca!

Lasca used to ride
On a mouse-grey mustang close to my side,
With blue serape and bright-belled spur;
I laughed with joy as I looked at her!
Little knew she of books or creeds;
An Ave Maria sufficed her needs;
Little she cared save to be at my side,

To ride with me, and ever to ride,
From San Saba's shore to Lavaca's tide.
She was as bold as the billows that beat,
She was as wild as the breezes that blow:
From her little head to her little feet,
She was swayed in her suppleness to and fro
By each gust of passion; a sapling pine
That grows on the edge of a Kansas bluff
And wars with the wind when the weather is rough,
Is like this Lasca, this love of mine.

She would hunger that I might eat,
Would take the bitter and leave me the sweet;
But once, when I made her jealous for fun
At something I whispered or looked or done,
One Sunday, in San Antonio,
To a glorious girl in the Alamo,
She drew from her garter a little dagger,
And—sting of a wasp—it made me stagger!
An inch to the left, or an inch to the right,
And I shouldn't be maundering here tonight;
But she sobbed, and sobbing, so quickly bound
Her torn rebosa about the wound
That I swiftly forgave her. Scratches don't count
In Texas, down by the Rio Grande.

Her eye was brown—a deep, deep brown;
Her hair was darker than her eye;
And something in her smile and frown,
Curled crimson lip and instep high,
Showed that there ran in each blue vein,
Mixed with the milder Aztec strain,
The vigorous vintage of Old Spain.
She was alive in every limb
With feeling, to the finger tips;
And when the sun is like a fire,
And sky one shining, soft sapphire
One does not drink in little sips.

The air was heavy, the night was hot,
I sat by her side and forgot, forgot;
Forgot the herd that were taking their rest,
Forgot that the air was close oppressed,
That the Texas norther comes sudden and soon,
In the dead of the night or the blaze of the noon;
That, once let the herd at its breath take fright,
Nothing on earth can stop their flight;
And woe to the rider, and woe to the steed,
That falls in front of their mad stampede!

Was that thunder? I grasped the cord
Of my swift mustang without a word.
I sprang to the saddle, and she clung behind.
Away! on a hot chase down the wind!
But never was fox-hunt half so hard,
And never was steed so little spared.
For we rode for our lives. You shall hear how we fared
In Texas, down by the Rio Grande.

The mustang flew, and we urged him on;
There was one chance left, and you have but one —
Halt, jump to the ground, and shoot your horse;
Crouch under his carcass, and take your chance;
And if the steers in their frantic course
Don't batter you both to pieces at once,
You may thank your star; if not, goodbye
To the quickening kiss and the long-drawn sigh,
And the open air and the open sky,
In Texas, down by the Rio Grande.

The cattle gained on us, and, just as I felt
For my old six-shooter behind in my belt,
Down came the mustang, and down came we,
Clinging together—and, what was the rest?
A body that spread itself on my breast,
Two arms that shielded my dizzy head,
Two lips that hard to my lips were prest;
Then came thunder in my ears,

As over us surged the sea of steers,
Blows that beat blood into my eyes,
And when I could rise —
Lasca was dead!

I gouged out a grave a few feet deep,
And there in the Earth's arms I laid her to sleep;
And there she is lying, and no one knows;
And the summer shines, and the winter snows;
For many a day the flowers have spread
A pall of petals over her head;
And the little grey hawk hangs aloft in the air,
And the sly coyote trots here and there,
And the black snake glides and glitters and slides
Into the rift of a cottonwood tree;
And the buzzard sails on,
And comes and is gone,
Stately and still, like a ship at sea.
And I wonder why I do not care
For the things that are, like the things that were.
Does half my heart lie buried there
In Texas, down by the Rio Grande?

"JUST A-RIDIN'!"

Oh, for me a horse and saddle
Every day without a change;
With the desert sun a-blazin'
On a hundred miles o' range,

Just a-ridin', just a-ridin',
Desert ripplin' in the sun,
Mountains blue along the skyline—
I don't envy anyone.

When my feet are in the stirrups
And my horse is on the bust;
When his hoofs are flashin' lightnin'
From a golden cloud o' dust;
And the bawlin' of the cattle
Is a-comin' down the wind—
Oh, a finer life than ridin'
Would be mighty hard to find,
Just a-ridin', just a-ridin',
Splittin' long cracks in the air,
Stirrin' up a baby cyclone,
Rootin' up the prickly pear.

I don't need no art exhibits
When the sunset does his best,
Paintin' everlastin' glories
On the mountains of the west.
And your operas look foolish
When the night bird starts his tune
And the desert's silver-mounted
By the kisses of the moon,

Just a-ridin', just a-ridin',
I don't envy kings nor czars
When the coyotes down the valley
Are a-singin' to the stars.

When my earthly trail is ended
And my final bacon curled,
And the last great round up's finished
At the Home Ranch of the world,
I don't want no harps or haloes,
Robes or other dress-up things—
Let me ride the starry ranges
On a pinto horse with wings,

Just a-ridin', just a-ridin',
Splittin' chunks o' wintry air,
With your feet froze to your stirrups
And a snowdrift in your hair.

"THE LEGEND OF BOASTFUL BILL"

At a round-up on the Gila
One sweet morning long ago,
Ten of us was throwed quite freely
By a hoss from Idaho.
An' we 'lowered he'd go a-beggin'
For a man to break his pride
Till, a-hitchin' up one leggin',
Boastful Bill cut loose an' cried:

"I'm a ornery proposition for to hurt,
I fulfil my earthly mission with a quirt,
I can ride the highest liver
'Twixt the Gulf an' Powder River,
An' I'll break this thing as easy as I'd flirt."

So Bill climbed the Northern fury
An' they mangled up the air
Till a native of Missouri
Would have owned the brag was fair.
Though the plunges kept him reelin'

An' the wind it flapped his shirt,
Loud above the hoss's squealin'
We could hear our friend assert:

"I'm the one to take such rockin's as a joke;
Someone hand me up the makin's of a smoke.
If you think my fame needs brightnin',
Why, I'll rope a streak o' lightnin'
An' spur it up an' quirt it till it's broke."

Then one caper of repulsion
Broke that hoss's back in two,
Cinches snapped in the convulsion,
Skyward man and saddle flew,
Up they mounted, never flaggin',
And we watched them through our tears,
While this last, thin bit o' braggin'
Came a-floatin' to our ears:

"If you ever watched my habits very close,
You would know I broke such rabbits by the gross.
I have kept my talent hidin',
I'm too good for earthly ridin',
So I'm off to bust the lightnin'—Adios!"

Years have passed since that ascension;
Boastful Bill ain't never lit;
So we reckon he's a-wrenchin'
Some celestial outlaw's bit.
When the night wind flaps our slickers,
And the rain is cold and stout,
And the lightnin' flares and flickers,
We can sometimes hear him shout:

"I'm a ridin' son o' thunder o' the sky,
I'm a broncho twistin' wonder on the fly.
Hey, you earthlin's, shut your winders,
We're a-rippin' clouds to flinders.
If this blue-eyed darlin' kicks at you, you die."

Star-dust on his chaps and saddle,
Scornful still of jar and jolt,
He'll come back sometime a-straddle
Of a bald-faced thunderbolt;
And the thin-skinned generation
Of that dim and distant day
Sure will stare with admiration
When they hear old Boastful say:

"I was first, as old raw-hiders all confest,
I'm the last of all rough riders, and the best.
Huh! you soft and dainty floaters
With your aeroplanes and motors,
Huh! are you the greatgrandchildren of the West?"

"THE DRUNKEN DESPERADO"

I'm wild and woolly and full of fleas,
I'm hard to curry below the knees,
I'm a she-wolf from Shamon Creek,
For I was dropped from a lightning streak
And it's my night to hollow—Whoo-pee!

I stayed in Texas till they runned me out,
Then in Bull Frog they chased me about,
I walked a little and rode some more,
For I've shot up a town before
And it's my night to hollow—Whoo-pee!

Give me room and turn me loose
I'm peaceable without excuse.
I never killed for profit or fun,
But riled, I'm a regular son of a gun
And it's my night to hollow—Whoo-pee!

Good-eye Jim will serve the crowd;
The rule goes here no sweetnin' 'lowered

And we'll drink now the Nixon kid,
For I rode to town and lifted the lid
And it's my night to hollow—Whoo-pee!

You can guess how quick a man must be,
For I killed eleven and wounded three;
And brothers and daddies aren't makin' a sound
Though they know where the kid is found
And it's my night to hollow—Whoo-pee!

When I get old and my aim aint true
And it's three to one and wounded, too,
I won't beg and claw the ground;
For I'll be dead before I'm found
When it's my night to hollow—Whoo-pee!

"THE END OF THE TRAIL"

Soh, Bossie, soh!
The water's handy heah,
The grass is plenty neah,
An' all the stars a-sparkle
Bekaze we drive no mo'—
We drive no mo'.

The long trail ends today, —
The long trail ends today,
The punchers go to play
And all you weary cattle
May sleep in peace for sure,—
May sleep in peace for sure,—

Sleep, sleep for sure.
The moon can't bite you heah,
Nor punchers fright you heah.
An' you-all will be beef befo'
We need you any mo'—
We need you any mo'!

"THE CAMPFIRE HAS GONE OUT"

Through progress of the railroads our occupation's gone;
So we will put ideas into words, our words into a song.
First comes the cowboy, he is pointed for the west;
Of all the pioneers I claim the cowboys are the best;
You will miss him on the round-up, it's gone, his merry shout,
The cowboy's left the country and the campfire has gone out.

There is the freighters, our companions, you've got to leave
this land,
Can't drag your loads for nothing through the gumbo and the
sand.
The railroads are bound to beat you when you do your level
best;
So give it up to the grangers and strike out for the west.
Bid them all adieu and give the merry shout,
The cowboy's left the country and the campfire has gone out.

When I think of those good old days, my eyes with tears do fill;
When I think of the tin can by the fire and the cayote on the hill.

I'll tell you, boys, in those days old-timers stood a show,
Our pockets full of money, not a sorrow did we know.
But things have changed now, we are poorly clothed and fed.
Our wagons are all broken and our ponies most all dead.
Soon we will leave this country, you'll hear the angels shout,
"Oh, here they come to Heaven, the campfire has gone out."

COWBOY GLOSSARY

Bad Lands—alkali, clayey, or desert land, poor or uncultivable.

Bad Man—outlaw.

Band—a very small herd of horses, cattle, sheep, or men on the range.

Beef Critter—a cattle heavy enough to be sold for beef.

Bit and Bridle

Bit—comprises mouthpiece, bit cheeks, and chains.

Bridle—comprises bridle cheeks or side leathers; brow band over eyes; throat latch, going around neck under ears and curb strap under jaw, all of which comprise the headstall which, with reins included, is considered a bridle.

Hackamore—comprises a bosal or rawhide loop noose over horse's nose with a light strap attached to each side and going over the head. A small, light five-to-sixteen-inch rope to give strength is attached to the knot, under-chin end of the bosal by special knots called *theodore knots*. From this junction this rope extends beyond the *theodore* knots and is used as a leading rope.

Hackamore Rope—is a rope by skillful looping of which a hackamore form of headplate is improvised.

Halter—a simplified headstall but usually of heavier leather without a brow band, used for tethering or leading, for which purpose a halter rope is attached.

Break Range—running off the range.

Breaking—conquering and taming and training a horse by force and fight.

Boys—cowboys or hands on a ranch.

Bronco Buster—a cowboy who rides and breaks wild or unbroken horses.

Buckaroo—or a broncho-buster—a cowboy who can ride and then some. Applied generally to the riders who take part in the roundup.

Bucking—gyrations of a horse to unseat a rider.

211

Bucking Straight Away—bucking that consists of long jumps straight ahead without twisting, whirling, or rearing. Usually not difficult for a buckaroo to ride.

Sunfishing—a movement which some bucking horses have, consisting particularly of a posterior twist, alternately left and right, as the animal bucks, so that the horse's body, when it rises in the air is in the form of an arc. A *sunfisher* is generally a very difficult animal to ride.

High Roller or High Poler—a horse that leaps high into the air when bucking.

Bucking-Horse Riding or Rough-Riding—riding untamed horses that buck.

Riding Slick—consists in riding with the usual cowboy equipment, i.e., saddle, chaps and spurs and without aid of hobbled stirrups, locked spurs, or bucking rolls.

Slick Heels—riding without spurs.

Locked Spurs—spurs in which rowels have been fastened so they will not move. When these spurs are held firmly in the cinch, it is impossible for a horse to unseat its rider. They are also barred.

Throwing the Steel—using the spurs, synonymous with raking and scratching.

Scratching—the act of a buckaroo while riding a bucking horse in using his spurs to make the animal buck its hardest. In scratching, the buckaroo must necessarily allow the legs to be free and thus take more chances. If a broncho-buster scratches a bad horse, he is generally making a good ride.

Raking—synonymous with scratching. Generally applies when rider gives his legs a free sweep, rolling the rowels of his spurs along the horse's side from shoulder to rump. Sometimes called scratching fore and aft. One of the highest accomplishments coveted by the broncho-buster.

Riding Straight Up—the rider of a bucking horse sitting erect in his saddle, one hand holding the halter rope and the other high in the air "fanning" with hat.

Close Seat—a seat in the saddle which is steady and firm. An important consideration in the eyes of the judges.

Riding Safe—sitting tight in the saddle, the legs tightly gripping the horse's sides and the spurs generally set firmly in the cinch.

Riding Sloppy—sitting loosely in the saddle, allowing body to wave and flop about in response to the gyrations of the animal. It is sometimes called "grandstand" riding but is not considered good form in a contest.

Seeing Daylight—a term applied when daylight can be seen between the rider and the seat of his saddle.

Pulling Leather—holding on to any part of the saddle, usually the horn, to steady oneself. A rider who pulls leather is in disgrace and is disqualified as surely as is one who is thrown. Most cowboys will allow themselves to be thrown before they will pull leather.

Choking the Biscuit—nearly synonymous with "pulling leather." Sometimes called *choking the horn*. Consists in catching hold of the horn of the saddle in order to keep from being thrown.

Biting the Dust—cowboy term for being thrown from a bucking horse and usually follows after "choking the biscuit." It also often happens to many hungry for adventure on the hurricane deck of a bucking bronc.

Bunch—applied to a small herd of horses or cattle or group of men.

Bunchgrassers—range horses living on bunchgrass.

Cattle Rustler—cattle thief.

Cattaloe—a hybrid offspring of a buffalo and a cattle.

Cavy—a band of saddle horses used on a roundup.

Chuck Wagon—cook wagon which accompanies an outfit of cowboys or others working on the range.

Cowboy or *Vaquero* (Sp.)—cowhand; ranch-hand, one of that adventurous class of herders and drovers of the plains and ranges of the western United States who does his work on horseback. He is famed for his hardiness, recklessness, and daring.

Critter—any man or beast.

Cut Out—to work out and separate animals from the herd.

Forty-Five—a .45 caliber revolver, usually a Colts or Smith & Wesson.

Gentling—any method of taming an unbroken or untrained horse.

Gypping—fooling or deceiving.

Highway Round—the natural way of living and dying.

Hitched—a pack, a horse, or anything tied up with a rope.

Hi-Yu-Skookum—Indian jargon used by Cayuse and Nez Perce tribes meaning "very good."

Hobbles—a short rope or any arrangement used for tying the fore fetlocks of a horse near together to prevent straying.

Honda—the mettle piece inside the eye splice of a lariat through which the noose of the rope travels.

Horse Rustler—horse thief.

Horses—often pronounced "hoss" or "hawse."

Broncho, Bronch, Bronc, or Bronk—a Spanish word applied to the small native Mexican horse meaning rough and wild, now applied to any untamed range horse.

Cayuse—an Indian pony; also the name of one of the tribes of Indians now located on the Umatilla reservation, members of which participate in the roundup.

Cuitan—Indian name for pony. Also called by cowboys bob-tail, fuzz-tail, and mustang.

Outlaw—sometimes called a "bad one" is a horse whose spirit is unconquerable and which can never be broken to ride. He always fights and always bucks. The animals ridden in the roundup bucking contests are outlaws of the worst type to be found in the world.

Slick-Ear—sometimes used synonymously with maverick but is usually applied to unbranded horses. Comes from the practice among early day horsemen of slitting the ears of their horses to distinguish them, so a horse with smooth or un-slit ears was as good as unbranded. A slick-ear can no more be claimed than a maverick.

Wild Horse—a native of the range that has never been ridden or broken. He may be a bucker or may not. The animals ridden in the wild horse race each day have never had more than a rope on them since the day of their birth. Many of them have seen but a few men in all their lives.

Jerk Water—applied to a little, insignificant place where trains stop only to take or jerk on water for the engine.

Lasher—man who handles the lash or whip on a stagecoach.

Lariat or Lasso—often called "rope" or "lass rope" made of plaited rawhide or hemp with a small loop or an eye splice shrunk over a brass honda at one end through which free end is run, thus forming the loop.

Mounting Pony Express—mounting to the saddle without the aid of the stirrups. Consists in the rider grabbing the horn of the saddle, starting his horse on a gallop, bounding two or three times by his side and leaping over the cantle into the seat. So called after the fashion of pony express riders in mounting to save time, or to show off.

Muck-A-Muck—Cayuse Indian jargon for food.

Mustang—see under horses.

Nestler—homesteader or squatter.

Outfit—a term applying to the equipment of man, horse, group of men, ranch, or a large concern, or to the men, horses themselves and to the complement of a ranch or concern or any group or part thereof.

'Onery—possibly an abbreviation for ornery, meaning mean, untractable, or worthless.

Passenger—in stagecoach race the cowboys who ride to balance coach to keep it from capsizing at the turns.

Pard—pardner, partner.

Peralta—the band or herd of cattle rounded up for cutting out.

Plum Cultus—expression meaning as bad as they make them, cussedest (*cultus* is an Indian word).

Posse—band of men organized to run down a man or a small band of men usually outlaws or thieves.

Quirt—see under saddle.

Ran a Butcher Shop and Got His Cattle Mixed—stole or rustled cattle and was found out.

Red Eye or Nose Paint—whiskey.

Rope—see "lasso."

Ropin'—lassooing.

Rough-Riding—riding a bucking horse.

Saddle—western saddle, cowboy saddle. This saddle is a distinct type comprising the following parts:

  Tree—a frame of wood covered with rawhide.

Horn—formerly of wood, now of steel, covered with rawhide.

Fork—the front part of the tree and supports horn.

Gullet—curved portion of underside of the fork.

Cantle—raised back to the saddle seat.

Side Jockeys—leather side extensions of seat.

Back Jockeys—top skirts the uppermost broad leathers joining behind cantle.

Skirts or *Suderderos* —(old Spanish) broad under leathers which go next to the horse.

Stirrup-Leathers—broad leathers hung from the bar of the tree and from which stirrups hang.

Strings—underlying purpose to hold saddle leathers together but ends are tied and left hanging, which adds to appearance as well as usefulness in tying on things carried.

Fenders or *Rosideros* —broad leather sweat protectors swinging from stirrup leathers.

Rigging—middle leathers attached to tree connecting with and supporting cinch by latigos through rigging ring.

Cinch or *Cincha* (Sp.)—a girth of horsehair, leather, cotton, or mohair strapped under horse's belly to cinch or hold the saddle on.

Rubber Cinch—an elastic cinch used in relay races to save time in changing saddles.

Cinch or Cincha Rings—on each end of the cinch.

Latigos—leather straps hanging from either side from the rigging ring, other ends run through cinch rings used to tighten up.

Stirrup—foot support usually of wood bound with iron or brass or rawhide, sometimes all iron or brass.

Hobbled Stirrups—stirrups tied to each other by a leather thong running under the horse's belly. With stirrups hobbled, it is almost the same as if the rider were tied in the saddle and there is no play to the stirrups. Hobbled stirrups are not allowed in bucking contests.

Tapideros or **Taps**—leather stirrup covers which serve as protection against cold and rain, especially through wet brush or grass, from eight to twenty inches in length. They are mostly for effect, though some claim the stirrups ride better. In summer they are discarded.

Quirt—a short heavy plaited pliable leather riding whip, used by cowboys.

Seat—the easiest thing to find on a saddle but the hardest to keep.

Scrub-Tail—see under horses.

Short Cut—hanging or shooting a man summarily.

Steer—young male of the ox kind, usually with wide-spreading horns especially raised for beef. In the western United States, one of any age. Range steers are dangerous to men on foot.

Maverick—an unbranded bullock or heifer. Said to be derived from the name of a Texas cattleman who neglected to brand his cattle.

Steer Bulldogging—a practice among cowboys consisting of wrestling with a steer barehanded. Usually the cowboy rides alongside the racing steer, leans over, seizes the horns of the animal, and swings to the ground. Then, using the horns as levers, he twists the head of the steer until its muzzle points upward, falls backward, thus throwing the steer off its balance. In exhibitions the cowboy fastens his teeth in the upper lip of the steer, releases the horns, and holds the animal prostrate with his teeth.

Hoolihanning—another form of bulldogging consists in forcing the horns of the running animal suddenly into the ground and thus turning the animal a complete somersault. However, this form is more dangerous to man and beast and is most cruel, inasmuch as the animal's horns are frequently broken.

Steer Busting—popular name for roping or throwing a steer with a lariat single handed.

Steer Roping—the art of capturing, busting, and hogtieing a range steer single-handed.

Hogtieing—tying together of the forefeet and one hind foot after a steer has been lassoed and thrown. The process must be quick in order to prevent the steer rising after he has been thrown.

Stick-Up Man—highwayman, stage robber.

Strays—cattle or horses which have mixed in with a herd but do not belong to it, or have wandered off from the herd.

Wanted—said of a man desired by the law.

Wind Bunch—any untamed herd of men, women, or horses.

Wrangling—rounding up, catching, and saddling range horses.

Wrangler—a buckaroo who handles the buckers in the arena and assists the rider in saddling his horse. This wrangling is often the most difficult and dangerous part of the task in subduing a wild horse.